MW00577523

New Orleans Vampires

Marita Woywod Crandle

Published by Haunted America
A Division of The History Press
Charleston, SC
www.historypress.net

Back cover: Photo courtesy of Mark Barrett.

First published 2017

Manufactured in the United States

ISBN 9781540226396

Library of Congress Control Number: 2017940960

This book is dedicated to those with
a thirst for knowledge
and a hunger for the truth.

Contents

Foreword

As a Stoker family historian and vampire enthusiast myself, I am so pleased to be writing this foreword for Marita. Her writing of this book evokes the memories of similar historical tales that my great-granduncle Bram Stoker became aware of during his lifetime.

For the past ten years I have been digging into some of the critical sources pertaining to my great-granduncle's writing of *Dracula*. I am fortunate enough to have been able to analyze his *Dracula* research notes in the Rosenbach Museum, his *Lost Journal* found in one of his great-grandsons' attic in a cottage on the Isle of Wight and, quite recently, the *Dracula Typescript* owned by Paul Allen. I feel like each of these treasures is a gift from the past pointing me in a direction to better understand my famous relative.

Published 120 years ago, *Dracula*, a classic, continues to evoke speculation from eager readers intrigued by the historical facts mixed with Bram's wonderful fiction. I lecture regularly at literary and film events—on the topic of the history and mysteries that surround *Dracula*—and always find that fans of the novel are genuinely interested in any background information I can provide.

I met Marita at a book signing of my own for *Dracula: The Un-Dead*, which she hosted at her vampire boutique. *Dracula: The Un-Dead* is a sequel to *Dracula* I coauthored in 2009. I saw the spark in Marita's eyes as she made my acquaintance, much like the enthusiasm I felt at discovering Bram's *Lost Journal*. To Marita, I was a link to the past. I could see that to her I was a "tell," insomuch as I was tied to all she was interested in, and the questions were mounting in her head. At the time, I did not know Marita's maiden name, nor did she know its significance to Romanian culture and her own tie to Vlad Dracula.

Reading through her *New Orleans Vampires: History and Legend* helped me remember that Bram Stoker had visited New Orleans with Sir Henry Irving and the Lyceum theater troupe in January 1896. I wonder just how much Bram became aware of local New Orleans history and folklore, much like he was drawn to similar horror stories in his native Ireland as a young boy. While he was writing *Dracula*, he focused on medieval accounts of what were thought to be real vampire-like creatures coming back from the dead from eastern European countries.

I am thrilled that Marita's curiosity about vampires and history has led to this book, which is a bit of a treasure itself for those intrigued by legends, as it unravels the interesting bits to make sense of the historical value yet leaves the mysteries of the legends intact.

The mere air of the French Quarter has one spinning with questions of the past. To a historian, New Orleans is like a candy store, having one gleaming in all directions and unsure which scrumptious piece to devour first. This book satisfies one's craving sweet tooth and carnivorous fangs!

—DACRE STOKER

Preface

I was about eight years old when my cousin Vera came to dinner at our house in California. Originally from Germany, my father moved our family to California a few years before that. Once we were settled, many other family members followed, and my cousin Vera was one of them. Vera, at the time, was president of a Crocker Bank branch close to our home. My cousin was giddy that evening with news from her day at the bank.

It seemed that a gentleman from Romania had business at the bank that required my cousin's attention. When he sat down at her desk and saw the nameplate in front of him, "Woywod," he immediately pushed back his chair and fell to his knees, bowing in front of her. Vera stood up to see what had happened. He respectfully avoided looking in her eyes as he said, "You are Queen of the gypsies!" He repeated this over and over, mixed with some Romanian words. Vera was stunned, standing there over him, not knowing what to do. She finally convinced him to return to his chair. It apparently took him some time to regain his composure, but eventually, they were able to make terms with his idea of her status and commenced with the business at hand. However, once their business was completed, he did make his exit from her office walking backward, bowing his way out the door. We all had a good laugh that night around the dinner table, and I didn't think of it again until about twenty-eight years later, after my move to New Orleans.

My father was very unhappy with my decision to move to New Orleans and give up my position as director of marketing for a conglomeration of companies, with home offices in California and Canada. The position offered a very attractive salary, diversity, travel and responsibility. I loved my job and my life in California, until that job sent me to New Orleans on business—a trip that changed my life forever.

My father found it impossible to understand why I would leave my house, my friends and my family to move to the French Quarter and tend bar and open—of all things—a vampire store. I must say, it was difficult to explain, because I didn't fully understand it myself. Some say Marie Laveau, the Voodoo Queen of New Orleans, had placed a spell on the city. Legend has it that her spell is all consuming, instilling a lust for returning to New Orleans to all those who visit here. Whether it was the curse of Marie Laveau, or simply the magical feel of everything New Orleans had to offer, I didn't feel it necessary to defend my decision. I simply forged ahead. It almost felt that the universe made the move for me, as everything fell exactly into place. I decided to stop questioning it and just enjoy the amazing adventure that was unfolding before me.

Then one day my father called with some incredulous news. My father was an avid reader and often followed the advice of the *New York Times* bestseller list, as many do. His interest was particularly peaked by a book titled *The Historian* by Elizabeth Kostova, as it was vampire themed. When he called, he let me know that a copy of the book was already on its way to me, and he urged me to read it as soon as it arrived. He explained in his excitement that in the book he had discovered that our family had ties to Vlad the Impaler, one of the most infamous "vampires" of all time. *The Historian* is a beautifully written book of historical fiction telling the story of a father and daughter in their quest to find Dracula, aka, Vlad Tepes.

Dracula is, of course, Bram Stoker's fictional character based on the Romanian leader Vlad Tepes. However, Voivode or Woywod Vlad Tepes was highly revered in Romania as a leader who ruled Wallachia with a fierce hand—a strong leader, king of the gypsies!

The dinner with my cousin Vera came flying back at me, slapping me in the face. "Queen of the Gypsies" indeed!

Shortly thereafter, my father delved deeper into research—and it's true. If you look up Vlad Tepes, as I have many times since, there is my maiden name staring me right in the face. Over the years, it has been modified various different ways, but our family name Woywod, pronounced "Voivot," is one of those modifications. I thought, what are the chances that the only girl in the country to open a vampire shop has a connection to one of the oldest vampire legends in existence?

Vlad Tepes, Voivode of Wallachia three times between 1448 and his death sometime between 1467 and 1477. *Public domain.*

Since I was very young, I, as many people, have enjoyed vampire legends, films, books—anything the creature offered. Often I dressed for Halloween as a vampire, as it allows you to still remain a bit glamourous, in a gothic way, yet appear dangerous. It also is a fairly simple costume to throw together, especially, when you have been naturally gifted with

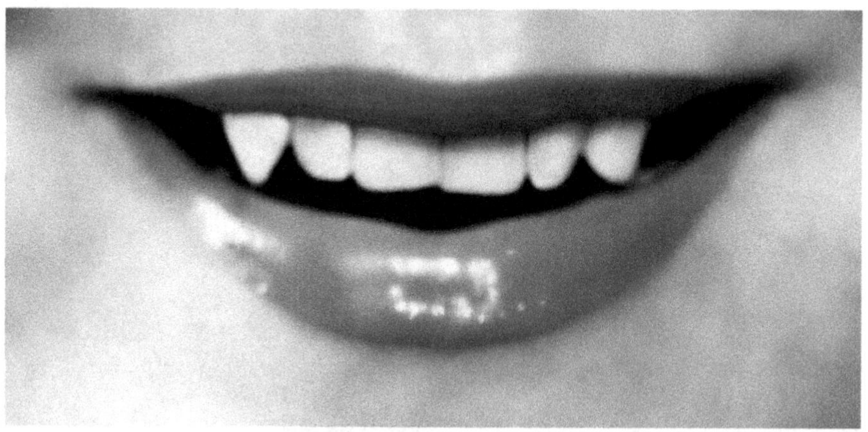

Author Marita Woywod Crandle's "fangs." *Photo by Linda Minutola Raymond.*

canines that are just pointy and long enough to resemble fangs. Another crazy coincidence, it really only came in handy around Halloween.

Otherwise, my fangs were really just bad teeth. However, once I opened the shop, I started to realize just how pronounced they were. Repeatedly, customers would ask to take pictures of my teeth and asked me if I had filed them or if I was wearing a set of our custom-made fangs. Often, people would come back with their entire family to show off my teeth. Our fangsmith, who creates custom fangs for our customers with dental acrylic, even matched to the color of their teeth, would often get customers asking to have teeth more like mine, instead of the options available on his sample poster. Customers would say that mine looked a little more realistic than his options—less assuming, yet still dangerous. I just learned to smile and chock it up to coming with the territory.

These are but two fantastical coincidences that leave even me wondering sometimes how all this just came about. This book is for all those people from all walks of life who have somehow been kissed by the vampire.

The world is a magical place. Stop asking questions of the magic, but don't hesitate to bask in it.

—MARITA WOYWOD CRANDLE

ACKNOWLEDGEMENTS

To my mother, Edda Woywod, for always encouraging my creative side and adding magic to my life.

To my husband for putting up with all my crazy ideas and for supporting and working with me on most of them.

To Russell Desmond of Arcadia books, for help with my French and for his wonderful guidance of where to look for what I needed.

To Emilie Leumas, archivist for the Archdiocese of New Orleans, for being so gracious with her time and generous with information and documents.

To Robert Ticknor, reference assistant, the Historic New Orleans Collection, Williams Research Center, for his kind spirit and extremely helpful information with research for this book.

To my editor, Amanda Irle, for making the work on this book a very fluid and fun experience.

To Anne Rice, for igniting my interest in New Orleans with her wonderful book *The Witching Hour*.

To Michael Machet, owner of Vampire Vineyards, for his support with all my projects.

To my friends Elaine Handloff, Alys Arden, Camille Burgin, Sue James, Kris Hammerquest, Nancy Deters and Nancy Morley for always encouraging me and supporting me with my vampire addiction and my writing.

Introduction

Fog rolls over the slates on the square just in front of the St. Louis Cathedral. Spilling onto the wrought-iron benches, the mist thickens while the sound of hooves clip the pavement, the mule leading its buggy into the distance. There's a reason Walt Disney fashioned his Magic Kingdom after the French Quarter in New Orleans. From the haunting buildings with Spanish lace balconies to the paddleboats floating down the Mississippi, from its bustling days with artists and musicians entertaining tourist on streets and in alleyways to its mystical nights with lovers dining in romantic restaurants and jazz from nightclubs flooding the streets, New Orleans has a magic you can find nowhere else. Perhaps that's why the magical are so drawn to the city. In addition to the romantic balconies, the music, the art, the rich history of brothels and pirates and its flourishing ports, there is also a mystical draw to the city with a darker side.

Witchcraft, voodoo and even vampirism have found their place in the French Quarter. There are several voodoo shops, some touristy, some authentic, offering guidance in the religion. There are witchcraft shops selling spells, potions and insight on the pagan religion and culture, and the only vampire shop in the country also found its home in the very heart of the French Quarter.

While voodoo and paganism are true religions, vampires, on the other hand, are mythical creatures that somehow draw those with a taste for the unknown. Vampires have a remarkable history. Tracing back to Egyptian hieroglyphics, most cultures have their own version of a creature that sustains

Left: Boutique du Vampyre Street sign at 709½ St. Ann. *Author's collection.*

Below: Eerie foggy morning in Jackson Square. *Courtesy of Mark Barrett.*

itself on human blood, a creature that draws one in, hypnotizing its victims and even promising eternal life to a select few. Super powers have been thought to give a vampire extraordinary speed and strength and possibly even the ability to fly and shift into bats, wolves and even fog, creating an allure around this creature that is enticing and even desirable.

When I first stepped foot in the French Quarter, I was not only mesmerized by the sensory overload the city offered, but I also knew

I was home. The pull to the city was unexplainable to even myself. I was spellbound, and like so many others, once I left, my heart ached to return. Maybe the pull that was tearing at my heartstrings was in fact the curse of Marie Laveau, the Voodoo Queen of New Orleans, instilling her all-consuming spell. As I walked through the streets, falling deeper and deeper under the spell, I imagined myself living here. All that was left was to devise a plan for my life in this magical place.

Author Anne Rice. *Wikimedia.*

Anne Rice brought such wonderful attention to New Orleans with *The Vampire Chronicles* series. I could immediately imagine her characters roaming the streets. I became intrigued with the news of a vampire tour on a pamphlet I picked up on a counter somewhere. Engaged in the tour, I followed the guide and listened to the legends of the vampires of the French Quarter, and it was at that moment that I imagined the success of a vampire-themed shop tucked away on one of the streets. A place where tourists could indulge in the mystery of the species. This crazy little city, in my mind, was probably the only place a shop such as this could survive.

I also found, just shortly after moving to the Quarter, that people migrate to the city to become whoever it is they really want to be. Many who move to the Quarter drop their given names and create an identity more suiting to their liking and desires. Those with a love for the nocturnal become fortune tellers, bartenders and tour guides, who in turn become vampire celebrities. It's the closest to living the life of a vampire that I could ever imagine.

Having owned Boutique du Vampyre for over fourteen years now, I have been privy to varying beliefs of a tremendous amount of people from all walks of life, including vampire identifiers, vampire aficionados, those who simply adore the creature and those who just find the shop too enticing to walk by without taking a look. Among all these visitors, I have come to the conclusion that almost everyone has some level of curiosity about the vampire. That combined with Anne Rice's popular vampires highlighting New Orleans as a vampire mecca build on visitors' curiosity of just why New Orleans has become synonymous with vampires.

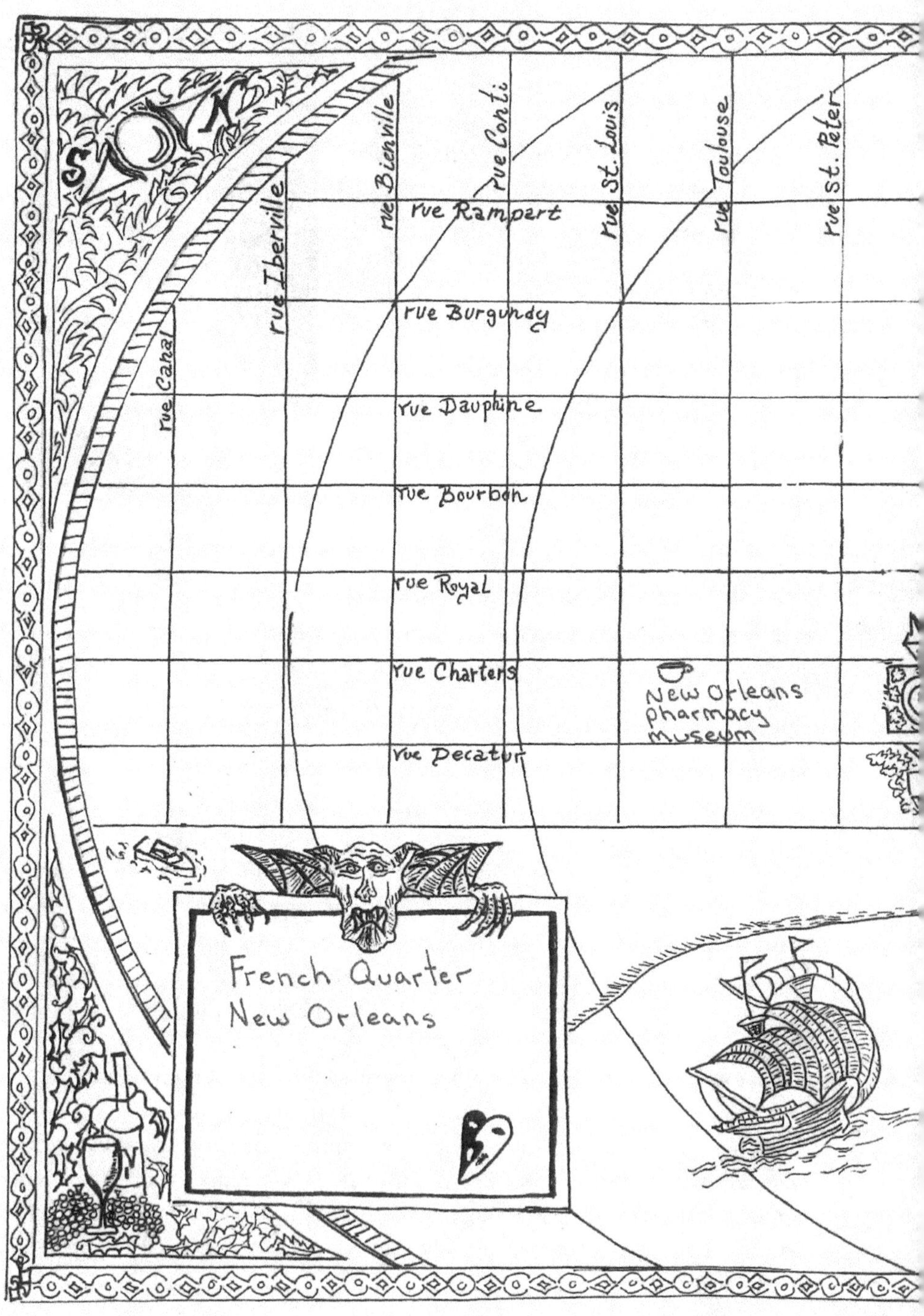

Illustration by author.

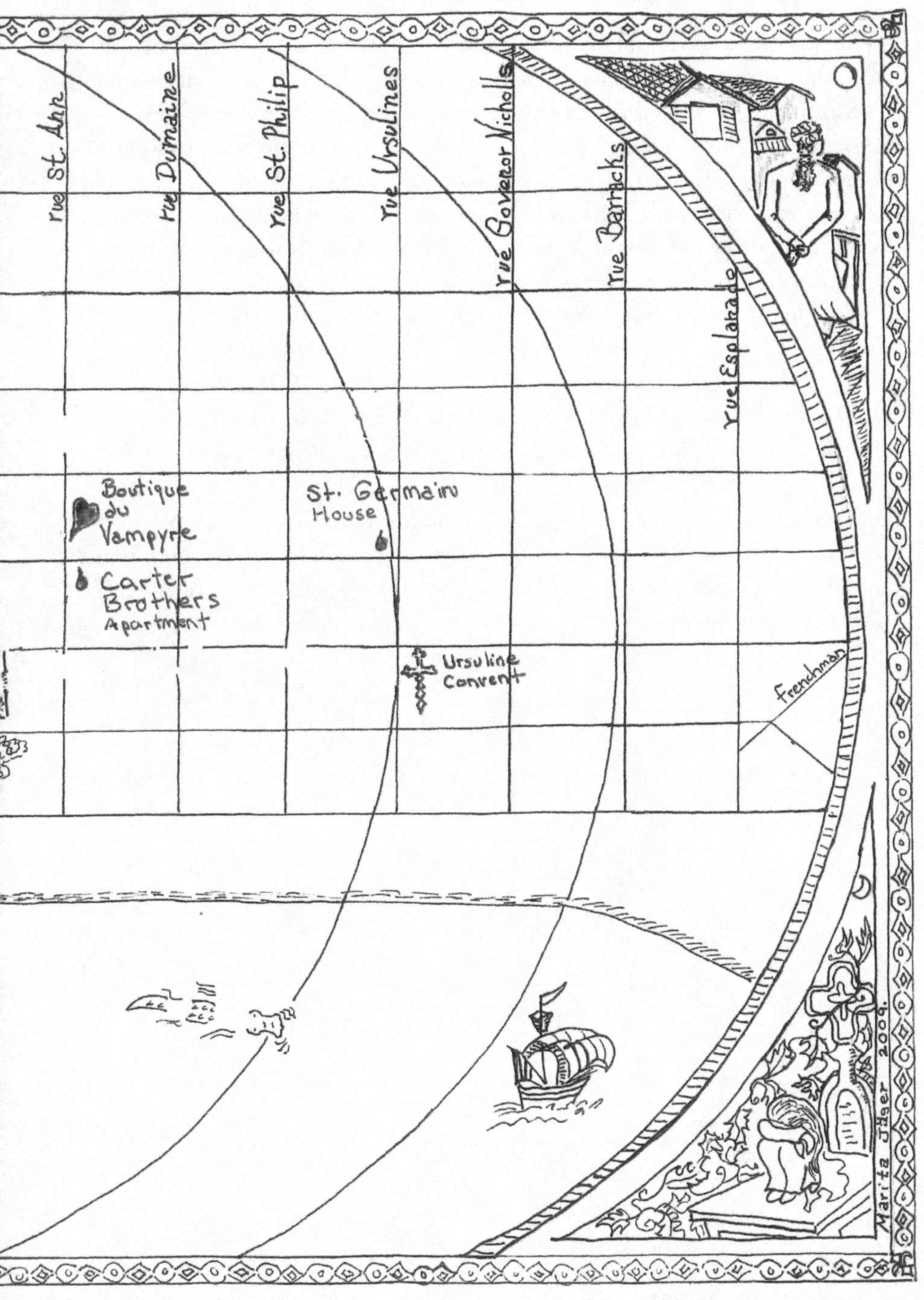
rue St. Ann
rue Dumaine
rue St. Philip
rue Ursulines
rue Governor Nicholls
rue Barracks
rue Esplanade
Boutique du Vampyre
Carter Brothers Apartment
St. Germain House
Ursuline Convent
Frenchman
Marita Jäger 2009.

The vampire tours highlight three legends in the French Quarter of people who either thought themselves to be vampires or, due to their suspicious behavior, those the city branded as vampires. Three stories, one from the 1700s, and two from the early 1900s, all permeate twelve mysterious square blocks. I personally have done a tremendous amount of research on all three legends, with the majority of the factual accounts being slim to none. However, the very definition of a legend is a story that is believed by many but cannot be proven. Many legends have some factuality behind them, such as Vlad the Impaler from Romania as the foundation for Bram Stoker's character Dracula. While my research proved thin, the legends and lore of French Quarter vampires remain.

In this book I will provide accounts of these legends in a way one would hope they be revealed, as campfire vampire lore. What you choose to believe or disbelieve will be left for you to discern. But for now, walk with me through the streets of the Quarter, reliving the tales of the creatures who roamed the nights. Let your imagination run wild, and in the end, you may find yourself gazing upon the sites where these legends were born with a taste for the mystery.

Part One

The Casket Girls

I

The Promised Land

Nightly, groups of tourists stand in the dark, across from the Old Ursuline Convent at 1100 Chartres Street, engaged in the legend of French vampire maidens held captive for close to three centuries in the third-floor attic. The third-floor dormer windows hold the fascination for this mystery, as their shutters remain tightly sealed. A unique circumstance, as no other top-floor shutters in the French Quarter can be found closed. Given that heat rises, in a city with intense humid temperatures, sealed windows would create an impossible situation for any source of comfort. A convent, ingénues from France and casket-shaped trousseaus stored in the mysterious attic become the ingredients of a vampire legend with a romantic twist.

Loose interpretation over the years has led to various versions of the legend, which begins in 1727 with a very select group of girls who sailed from France to New Orleans under the care of the Ursuline nuns. The girls were intended to be married off to men who had migrated south, spawning Louisiana's colonization. It's said the girls traveled with curious, coffin-shaped trousseaus, which earned them the nickname "Casket Girls." The hope was that these girls would help tame the city and populate it with a better class of people, as New Orleans had become a cluster of criminals and degenerates. However, on the ship many people became very ill, and several even died. According to the legend, the girls unknowingly smuggled vampires onto the ship in their trousseaus. The dark quarters of the ship kept whatever evil aboard comfortable throughout the journey. One by one, the maidens were being turned into

Tour group in front of the Ursuline convent. *Author's collection.*

creatures of the night for companionship. The vampires then feasted on the other passengers for survival.

Over the course of the bloody dark, long and gruesome journey to New Orleans, the Ursulines are said to have won the battle against the vampires with the holy power of God. However, they were bound in their responsibilities to protect the girls. Upon their arrival to New Orleans, they are said to have secured the maidens, eternally under their care, in the Ursuline convent attic to ensure mortal safety, as the girls were now fully turned vampire. Every window on the third floor was then sealed shut with a series of blessed screws to further ensure their captivity. Now and then stories are told of a shutter popping open on a gloomy night, possibly from the power of a vampire, longing for a glimpse of reality. However, it's said the monsignor, who has sole access to the third-floor chambers, immediately secures the shutters once again with more blessed screws, sealing the vampires safely from the world they would surely terrorize and destroy.

A great deal of confusion and mystery surrounds this legend. While the elements are all present in the historical facts, they simply don't line up. Yes, the convent's shutters remain closed, and the Ursuline nuns are famous for their great care in teaching and nurturing the development of women throughout the centuries; and yes, girls were sent from France to help populate New Orleans at the dawn of the city's colonization. However, should someone with interest investigate the story further, the mystery begins to unravel. A flurry of facts flutter unconnected around the legend, lending even more intrigue to this mystery.

The vast confusion stems from the fact that many past historians, in their documentations, writings and notes, were themselves at fault for making several mistakes, assumptions and careless recollections on the topic of the Casket Girls. Later, their documents were referred to and used as facts for future writings until the resulting story could be considered a product of "Chinese whispers" or "the telephone game." One person says this, and it is embellished to that, which goes on to be considered a different version of this. Historians making careless mistakes, coupled with French to English translation nuances, are at the root of the confusion surrounding the meat of this story. Luckily, ample documentation on the topic still exists, so the truth can be pieced back together.

It all began at the time when explorers were still traveling the world, discovering new territories to claim for their leaders. In these exciting and mysterious times, adventurers used any available means to accomplish their goals, some innovative, some unethical and even ruthless.

Originally from what is now Montreal, Quebec, Canada, French explorer Pierre Lemoyne d'Iberville was destined for priesthood. However, at the age of just twelve, his destiny took a dramatic turn when he secured a job as a cabin boy on his uncle's ship. This action steered him into a life of an adventurer, which lead to critical contributions to American history, including the founding of Louisiana. It is with his story that the making of our legend begins.

From the time that d'Iberville founded the colony of Le Nouvel Orleans in 1699, on numerous occasions he pleaded with the French government to send marriageable young women, preferably somewhat attractive, to tame and satisfy the tastes of the strong Canadian men who were to help colonize New Orleans. The girls were to be married off to them immediately upon their arrival. Iberville believed, quite wisely, and in the fashion of King Louis XV of France who used similar tactics several years prior, that it was crucial to the successful colonization of the new territory to bring families and women for men to marry, so to help root the men and start real cities in the territory.

Many of the men were *Coureur des bois*, French-Canadian woodsmen, who engaged in less traditional fur trade. The men would go deep into the woods to trade European items for furs. The original hope had been that these men would colonize with Indian women, but that wish turned out to be futile, as the Indians did not favorably adopt the ways of the French. Rather, the woodsmen adopted the very relaxed lifestyle of the Indian women, inhibiting the growth of the colony. Sending French women became a priority.

Pierre Lemoyne d'Iberville. *Public domain.*

To appease their needs, forty women were sent on the ship *Pelican* in 1704. However, the handful of women was little more than a temporary solution to the situation. The competition for the few women sent created a constant pressure for more women. The women were frankly needed not just to populate the colony but to keep the men interested in agriculture and other jobs that required their continual presence in New Orleans, when their nature had them seeking adventures and wandering.

At this time, John Law and his Western Company, which later became the Company of the Indies, were hired to populate the new territory. Ruthless, his men, as noted in Walter Hart Blumenthal's book *Brides from Brideswell*,

> *spared no violence in kidnapping city scourings and unsophisticated peasants. Vagrants, beggars, disorderly soldiers, galley-slaves, gipsies, paupers, prostitutes, political suspects, black sheep of good families, felons, were herded afoot or in carts under vigilant guard to a seaport and crowded aboard a ship in cramped quarters to fill up the then vast void of Louisiana.*

Blumenthal's intent for his book was to draw attention to a primarily overlooked group of individuals who also hold the status of America's ancestors. While much attention in American history had been given to *Mayflower* descendants as the foundation for the country, there was a much more diabolical colonization taking place a little farther south.

Several ships were sent to the promised land with a flood of women. While French, they were of a much less desirable nature than those on the *Pelican*. Some traveled willingly, misled by promises of abundant crops, meat and friendly Indians, expecting a modest but comfortable life. An advertisement was even circulated depicting Louisiana as a paradise of sorts, with lush territory, mountains and opportunity. (See insert.) Others were kidnapped and forced against their will, and some were bound in chains, already planned for deportation from France for their crimes, including murder, prostitution and thievery. Many were also exhibiting the early stages of gonorrhea, among other various diseases. This clan of hoodlum women were anything but desirable, and many died en route or shortly after their arrival. The legend of the Casket Girls cites a high death toll aboard the ship as evidence that the girls were feasting on their fellow passengers, but that rumor likely stems from all the horrid conditions and ill spirits the women who were shipped to New Orleans endured. There is nothing, however, to substantiate that one ship suffered more deaths than any other sent to Louisiana.

Women who did survive the journey were left in shock at the condition of Louisiana. The atmosphere of what was to be their new home was truly devastating. Many lived in hunger, with next to no vegetation, livestock, butter or any nutrition they were familiar with, and even accustomed to, in France. The accommodations were no more than primitive huts, void of most furnishings, utensils or any sign of civilization. Starving and depressed, few survived the experience, proving that the compromising efforts to send just any women were little more than good intentions.

However, shortly thereafter, one more attempt was made with twelve very unattractive girls who had little supervision on the ship during their travels. Their freedom on the ship, coupled with abundant idle time, had them engaged in less desirable behavior for young maidens who were to be wed. Deflowered, along with looks that apparently had the Canadian men running back into the woods, these girls proved once again the need for sending French women of a higher status—French women who could keep a man engaged and working in a fashion that would support the lifestyle of a French lady. These unfortunate women were thrown into a hard, loveless life in the swampy territory scavenging for survival, and most, if not all, soon succumbed to their fates.

It was at this time that the last group of marriageable girls, who became known as the Casket Girls, were shipped to New Orleans on the cargo ship *La Baleine* on January 8, 1721. The Casket Girls, or cassette girls, were said to have been carefully handpicked from the group of orphans housed at La Salpêtrière, a home for the poor of Paris at the time. They were called the *filles du cassette*, meaning "girls of cassettes," cassettes being small dowries filled with items that would increase their desirability for quick marriage. These dowries were small suitcases. However, because the French name for these suitcases is cassette, this become a juicy part of the legend. Americans heard the suitcases the girls traveled with referred to as cassettes and even caskets, so they fantasized that the girls traveled with caskets, or coffin-shaped suitcases. This, of course, was not true.

These young women have also been confused with *filles du roi*, "girls of the king," who were a select group of girls, also orphans, brought by King XIV to Quebec from 1663 to 1673. The King of France acted as their guardian, taking them under his wing as they were sent on to Quebec to be married and help colonize New France. These girls were of fine virtue and treated as such. They were given dowries and granted fifty livres, a handsome sum at the time.

Much like many Americans have proudly linked their lineage to passengers of the *Mayflower*, some in the South have boasted of being descendants of the Casket Girls. These girls were thought of as handpicked maidens of virtue, closely cossetted by the Ursuline nuns until married to start the colonization of Louisiana. Unfortunately, this romantic story has a treacherous truth. Some of that confusion most likely originated with the misunderstanding of the filles du roi and filles du cassette as one in the same, thus giving people a false sense of their ancestors' status. While the filles du roi were the predecessors of the cassette girls, they were afforded many luxuries the cassette girls were not. The king was not involved in sending the cassette girls to Louisiana. Rather it was organized by a private organization, the Company of the Indies. Although organizers followed the general system of the king's, the plan for the cassette girls was poorly executed.

Accounts conflict as to how many Casket Girls journeyed on *La Baleine* to America, with numbers varying anywhere from ninety to five hundred. The most accurate account is a list found in the National Genealogical Society Quarterly (which was taken from the Archives Nationales in Paris, France), listing eighty-eight girls, all of whom came from the Hôpital-General de la Salpêtrière, a house of detention with a chilling reputation. The hospital of sorts hosted orphan girls along with hopeless and homeless young women, prisoners, prostitutes, epileptics and the insane. The cassette girls were among these and around two dozen in number, orphans between fourteen and seventeen years old who sailed accompanied by a chaperone, Sister Gertrude, and two other sisters, Louise and Berge're. The other sixty or so women were of less virtue, prostitutes and criminals who had also previously been housed at la Salpêtrière. They did not travel with trousseaus or chaperones; that luxury was reserved for the young handpicked maidens

The Casket Girls traveling to New Orleans. *Courtesy Office of Archives and Records, Archdiocese of New Orleans.*

under the sisters' supervision. The other women were nothing more than prisoners being deported from France.

In the book *Fleur de Lys and Calumet*—the translated memoirs of Andrea Penicaut, who was coined "Louisiana's first historian" and chosen to join d'Iberville's expedition to establish Louisiana—Penicaut reports that the girls' trousseaus included "two suits of clothing, two skirts, and petticoats, six laced bodices, six chemises, six headdresses, and all other necessary accessories, with which they were well provided so that they could be married as quickly as possible in legitimate wedlock."

Historian Alcee Fortier then, in his "A History of Louisiana," makes three assumptions in one statement that can be traced directly back to where much of the confusion of the Casket Girls began. He writes:

> *In 1728 a ship had arrived with young girls who were to be married to the colonists. Each girl had received a small casket containing some articles of clothing, and they were known afterwards as les filles a las cassette. They were of good character, and were placed under the charge of the Ursuline Nuns until their marriage.*

Fortier uses the term *casket* here in reference to the small trousseaus the girls traveled with. In the *Pocket Oxford Dictionary*, casket's first usage is as follows: "small box often of costly make for valuables"; second usage, "U.S. only—coffin." This misunderstanding allowed Americans' imaginations to fantasize of what the girls might have transported in caskets from France.

Alcee Fortier, in his writings, makes the mistake of assuming that the nuns the girls traveled with were Ursulines, when they were not. They were Sisters from la Salpêtrière, who sailed with these girls six years prior to the Ursulines' journey to Louisiana. Furthermore, he makes the mistake of assuming the girls sailed in 1728, when the Ursulines had sailed to Louisiana. Rather, as is documented in a passenger list from the ship *La Baleine*, the girls sailed in 1721. The cassette girls were on the ship *La Baleine*, and *La Baleine* did sail to Louisiana again in 1728; however, there is no mention of any girls or Ursulines aboard that ship. Rather, that ship brought a packet of important letters to the church. The Ursulines had no orphans in their care during their 1728 journey to New Orleans and sailed on the ship *Gironde*.

La Baleine was a small French flute cargo vessel, and while there is no passenger list on record, the following is what has been accepted as a substitute.

French flute ship, circa 1720. *Public domain.*

Names of the girls from the Maison de St. Louis,
Of the Salpetriere, who have been remitted
To the Sieurs De Lage and Betouzet, Constabulary Guards
On 12 June 1720, to be conducted to Painbeuf
Where they are to embark for Louisiana.
(F5b:54, Archives Nationales, Paris, France)

Name	**Age**
Bled, Marie	20
Masson, Marguerite	21
Le Roy, Marie Louise	20
Follet, Madeleine	25
Morline, Genevieve	18
Mercier, Marie Madeleine	16
Heriot, Margeurite Claude	18
Maroy, Marie Françoise	17
Late, Melanye	18
Fetique, Marie Anne	13
François, Marie	22
Le Noble, Jeanne	15
Huly, Thoinette	26
Godefroy, Marie Jeanee	22
Claircatoire, Marie	20
Jelain, Marie Jeanne	24
Charlotte, Marie Anne	20
Le Comte, Barbe	13
Le Mire, Louise	16
Boulogne, Madeleine	19
Grandval, Gabriel(le)	20
Blanchard, Catherine	18
Boyer, Genevieve	25
Muguet, Marie Françoise	19
Gento, Anthoinette	18
Melier, Catherine	18
Lembajoye, Marie	18
Le Moine, Marie Claude	18
Belanger, Margueritte	26
Denis, Margueritte	23
Goneau *dite* Rose, Marie Anne	26

Le Tillier, Marie Louise	17
Leveille, Marie Therese	18
Rabu, Françoise	25
Vollery, Louise	17
Lese, Louise Benedic	18
Legain, Louise	23
Billard, Genevieve	17
Burei, Marthe	21
Bady, Catherine	20
Dubuisson, Marie Gabriel	18
Du Bis, Catherine Barbe	22
Bocquet, Marie	22
Dumont, Thoinon	21
Blegnot, Marie Jeanne	17
Pegnard, Jacqueline	25
Richard, Marie Louise	16
Nayon, Marie Anne	25
Lange, Anne	18
Le Jeune, Marie Marguerite	16
Mavre, Genevieve	15
Madou, Jeanne	15
Foucalt, Marie Anne	17
Daudessot, Marie Anne	28
Le Grand, Marie Jeanne	20
La Pleine, Marie	19
Couturier, Charlotte	12
Le Brun, Marie	17
Briere, Heleine	14
Chevet, Jeanne	15
Foucaut, Marie Catherine	18
Beganies, Marguerite	15
Vigernon, Anne	30
Menu, Catherine	28
Vaillet, Perrette	18
Bloy, Agnes	18
Duvet, Marguerite	17
Giraudon, Marie Anne	21
Girard, Angelique	22

Florant, Marie Angelique	23
Villeroy, Marie	17
Hubert, Jeanee	18
Aleaume *dite* Voillot, Denise	18
Clavier, Elizabeth	17
Savary, Françoise	20
Girard, Elizabeth	17
Paule, Catherine	23
Cordier, Marie Madeleine	21
Laurent, Marie Catherine	17
Hubrt, Catherine	22
Desrost, Genevieve	25
Gauzalau, Catherine	19
Garnier, Marie Genevieve	16
Kenel Marie	18
Manny, Anne	19
De Launey, Elisabeth	18
Chevalier, Catherine	14
Maisonnette, Therese	20
Jamart, Marie Anne	16

We the undersigned constabulary guards recognize that the girls named in the present statement have been remitted to our care, to be conducted to Painbeuf, where we are to remit them to the captain of the flute La Baleine *on which the girls are to be embarked; and we are to report to the Company of the Indies for our discharge and recognizance by the captain that the said girls have been remitted to him. Done at Paris, 12 June 1720.*
(signed) Delage Betouzet

Leaving from Nantes, the girls faced grisly conditions, coupled with the uncertainty of their fate upon their arrival. Travel at the time depended greatly on the winds, and with less-than-accurate charts, courses were haphazard and brutal. The threats of pirates and enemy warships were constant and provoked fear and uncertainty among the crew and passengers. The accommodations were dark and damp, with no privacy, including the lack of a changing room, causing most passengers to remain in the same clothes throughout their journey. The deck was the only real social area, where meals would also be taken, if weather permitted. At night, the ship was pitch black, as no candles or lanterns were permitted for fear of fire. The meal rations were always less than adequate, consisting of biscuits, some vegetables and soups and cod or salted meats available for dinner. The lack of vitamins combined with the small rations often led to illness and even starvation.

Upon their arrival, bachelors were encouraged to attend gatherings, where the girls were made readily available to select for marriage. It is reported in the writings of Andrea Penicaut that these girls, while still not as pretty as d'Iberville had requested, were kept behind lock and key at night in their temporary accommodations and strictly supervised by Sister Gertrude so as to retain their virtue. The hope was that these girls would enter into sound marriages to positively proceed with the much needed colonization in the new territory, after so many other attempts with less virtuous women had failed. The girls who had sailed on *La Baleine* thus also became known as the Baleine Brides. They were monitored much more carefully than their predecessors and were basically ensured to be virgins. Many references are made to the poor character of their chaperone, Sister Gertrude, by her supervisors, as noted in documents written by d'Iberville.

Arrival of the Ursulines in New Orleans, charcoal by Madeleine Hachard, circa 1727. *Courtesy of the Office of Archives and Records, Archdiocese of New Orleans.*

The sister, one of the officers of la Salpêtrière, was apparently sent away just three months after their arrival, shortly after most of the girls had been married. Governor Jean-Baptiste Le Moyne de Bienville wrote from Biloxi, regarding the nun, that "she rules sourly and capriciously, and has been guilty of a prank, which has cost her the respect of the girls themselves." It must have been a truly terrifying experience for these girls, first raised in la Salpêtrière, which provided its own horrors, then the gruesome ship's voyage along with constant threats of attack, in the care of a guardian who was less than comforting, all ending with landing in a very primitive territory to be married to a woodsman. These are girls with such colorful experiences that invite the manifestation of legends.

Over the years, various versions of the girls' perilous journey emerged, and eventually, the rumor of orphan girls from France transporting coffin-shaped trousseaus to the Ursuline convent was spread among locals and then retold as legend to those visiting the French Quarter. However, given all the facts that make it easy to debunk the legend, there remain curiosities to question. For instance, although the convent may never have housed any of the Casket Girls, the convent's mysterious attic remains sealed tight even to this day. It would be crucial at this point to investigate the travels of the Ursuline nuns to New Orleans, along with their business in New Orleans upon their arrival in this mystery that has them holding the girls hostage in the ominous attic.

2

The Ursulines Journey South

Twelve Ursuline nuns left France in 1727 to journey to New Orleans at the direction of King Louis XV of France. Embarking on a three-month voyage that turned into five grueling months at sea, the nuns were to open a convent that would see to the sick of the city and serve as a school to educate the young women of families with means as well as women and young girls in all desperate situations. Their journey, a long, unpleasant one, had them eager to begin their work upon their arrival. The convent, still under construction, found the nuns housed in one of the larger homes in the French Quarter, doing their work and awaiting their permanent accommodations.

Just as desperately as d'Iberville had requested marriageable women for the colonization of Louisiana, he simultaneously requested Grey Sisters (Daughters of Charity, Servants of the Sick Poor) to come to the aid of the hospital in New Orleans. It was a blessing when the Ursulines agreed to send twelve nuns to New Orleans to tend to the desperate needs of the sick when no other Catholic nuns could be convinced to take the charge, primarily because they were spread extremely thin with the needs at hand in France. However, the Ursulines asked that in return they be granted a convent for the schooling of young women, as was their constant charge. Sister Marie Madeleine Hachard, at the request of her father, recounted her journey in five lengthy letters during her travels, now historical treasures. It was extremely fortunate for historians that Hachard was not yet a fully professed nun, which enabled her to stay in contact with her family. These letters are fascinating in that they not only explain, in detail, the events as they occurred, they also are penned with the sister's heart and soul, giving the reader special insight into what these determined, God-adoring, feminine, yet tenacious, pioneers truly endured throughout their journey and the countless challenging situations they conquered.

The nuns' journey to Louisiana began with incredulous circumstances, and the remainder of the trip did not disappoint in the avenue of adventure. The ship awaiting them, the *Gironde*, was very tall and impossible to access in a civilized manner, so the nuns were put two at a time in cargo bags and hauled up the side of the ship with a pulley. Sister Hachard's attitude throughout the journey, and that of the nuns who were her superiors, are to be admired and revered. In the letters, Sister Hachard writes about dreadful nights spent waiting in the dark on meager bunks in anticipation of assisting the crew should pirates attack. Yearning to near the Mississippi and finally see land, they were left in terror as their ship nearly sank when it hit land. The captain had them throw sugar, wine and other supplies overboard to free the ship so that the passengers might keep their own belongings. Sister Hachard confesses that the fear of death ran through her. One might say these women quickly earned the title of adventurer in addition to that of their current status as servants of the Lord. Once their ship finally landed on Dauphine Island, they went to Belize, a spot just at the mouth of the Mississippi, which is no longer there. From Belize, they spent seven days traveling by pirogue to New Orleans through mosquito-filled nights with no shelter from the imminent storms. The exasperating journey to New Orleans showed their courageous nature, and it is remarkable that Sister Hachard writes that while troubled at the time, she thinks back pleasurably on each catastrophic event as little adventures.

Upon their arrival to New Orleans, the nuns were graciously received and temporarily housed directly on the opposite end of the city from the hospital, at a home Sister Hachard describes glowingly as one of the most beautiful in the city, writing to her father that it was more than they needed. The nuns were cloistered and not able to walk about town, so accessing the hospital across town to aid the sick was impossible. Thus, to the nuns' good fortune, they were immediately able to begin teaching young girls, as was their desire. They not only taught school basics, but they also taught girls how to cook and sew.

While their convent was being built, the nuns were boarding a variety of students and also teaching day classes. They were approached about also taking in and reforming women prisoners. Thus, there would be an additional apartment built for these women, attached somewhere to the convent. Hachard writes to her father that the hope is to move to the convent sometime in 1729—several years after the cassette girls arrived in Biloxi. In fact, in her letters, while she writes of many orphans, savages and black youth, Sister Hachard never mentions schooling or boarding at their home or convent these girls from France. Rather, the girls that she often refers to are either from Canada or Belize.

The legend of the Casket Girls owes much to historian Alcee Fortier's erroneous assumptions, discussed in the previous chapter, which have generally been interpreted as fact, as many of the elements surrounding them did occur.

Even more confusion comes into play with the book *Fleur de Lys and Calumet*, by Richebourg Gaillard McWilliams, the translated *Penicaut Narrative*, which is known as the earliest documentation of the French colonization of Louisiana, written in 1723 by Andre Joseph Penigault. McWilliams also makes an incorrect assumption in a footnote:

> *These are not the so-called cassette girls, who came to Louisiana in 1718, although these girls are similarly provided. There is great contrast in the provenience of the two shipments. These girls, Penicaut says, had been brought up in la Salpêtrière from infancy. They must have been the abandoned children—orphans or illegitimates—of prostitutes or "kept" women who had been inmates in that house of correction.*

However, McWilliams was mistaking the cassette girls for the women who were shipped over earlier, in 1718, under John Law's Western Company's corralling of degenerates. He also refers to what he believes to have been Ursuline nuns as Grey Sisters, which they were not.

Another reference to the girls is made in Jean Delanglez's *The French Jesuits in Lower Louisiana.* In an endnote, he asserts, "No 'Gray Sisters' accompanied those girls, for there seems to be an error in LA Harpe, 85. Three sisters—Gertrude, Louise and Bergere accompanied ninety-six filles de la salpetriere but this was in 1721." The "La Harpe" that Delanglez refers to here is a journal, *L'etablissement des Francais a la Louisiane*, or *Historical Journal of the Establishment of the French in Louisiana*, which is yet another document with conflicting information. There is much criticism of La Harpe's recollections in his journal, believed to be fabricated or embellished. Regarding the cassette girls, he is careless in his facts regarding only the dates and the assumption that the girls sailed with Ursulines.

These conflicting accounts on the topic of the Casket Girls were simply carelessness on the part of the historians and created the confusion about who these girls were and when they actually arrived. However, after sifting through the information, it is now clear that the Baleine Brides were, in fact, the cassette girls, later known as Casket Girls, who sailed to Louisiana under the care of the sisters of la Salpêtrière, and most likely were directed to Biloxi. However, the girls might have migrated independently to many different areas of Louisiana thereafter. The Ursulines then arrived in 1728, many years after the Casket Girls landed in Louisiana.

The first Ursuline convent wasn't completed until 1734, on the property at 1100 Ursuline. It is at that time that the nuns went by procession to claim their new home. It was unusual and a bold move, as tradition would have them travel in covered carriages to respect their cloistering. The nuns rather wished to demonstrate their status as pillars of the community,

The St. Louis Cathedral illustration. *The Collins C. Diboll Vieux Carre' Digital Survey at the Historic New Orleans Collection, N-218.*

marching confidently through the city across Jackson Square, in front of the St. Louis Cathedral, with students dressed as angels, followed by nuns. A few who held the most revered positions were completely concealed by canopies. It was after this that the nuns were able to help with the ill, as promised. However, teaching remained their focus. The procession makes for an interesting twist for the legend, as had the Ursulines been charged with holding the vampire maidens captive, they could have trafficked them in caskets to the convent, securely behind canopies, to their permanent home in the attic. With the distraction of the procession, the nuns might have made the celebration their salvation.

In Louisiana's infancy, under the poor populating efforts of John Law, the morale of the immigrants—most of whom were shipped against their will to swampy territory—was mediocre, and the future of the territory was questionable. The arrival of the Ursuline nuns was a significant and pivotal point in Louisiana history, as their effect on the people brought a civilized tone, faith and structure to a city that had been a bastion of deceit and corruption.

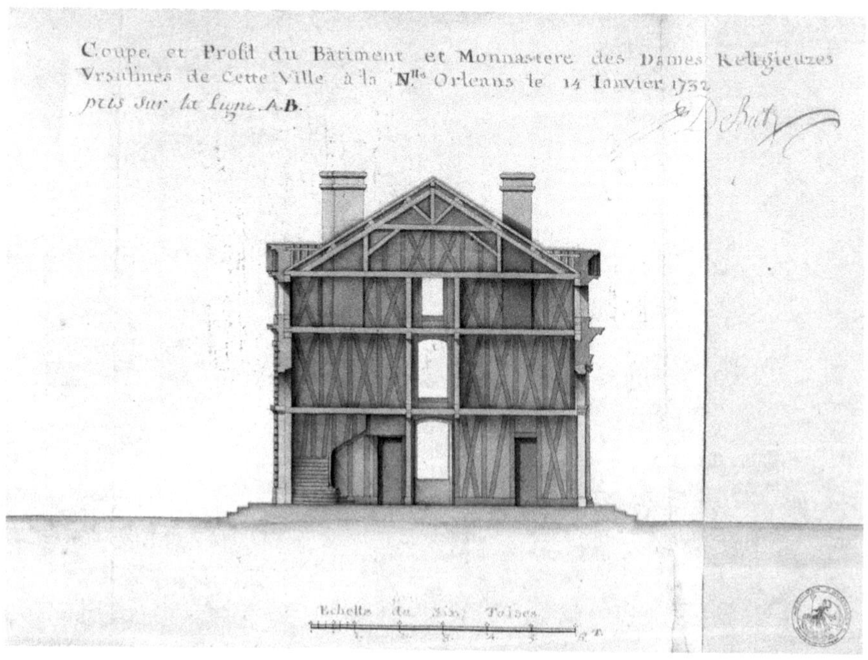

Architectural plans for first Ursuline's Convent. *Courtesy of the Office of Archives and Records Archdiocese of New Orleans.*

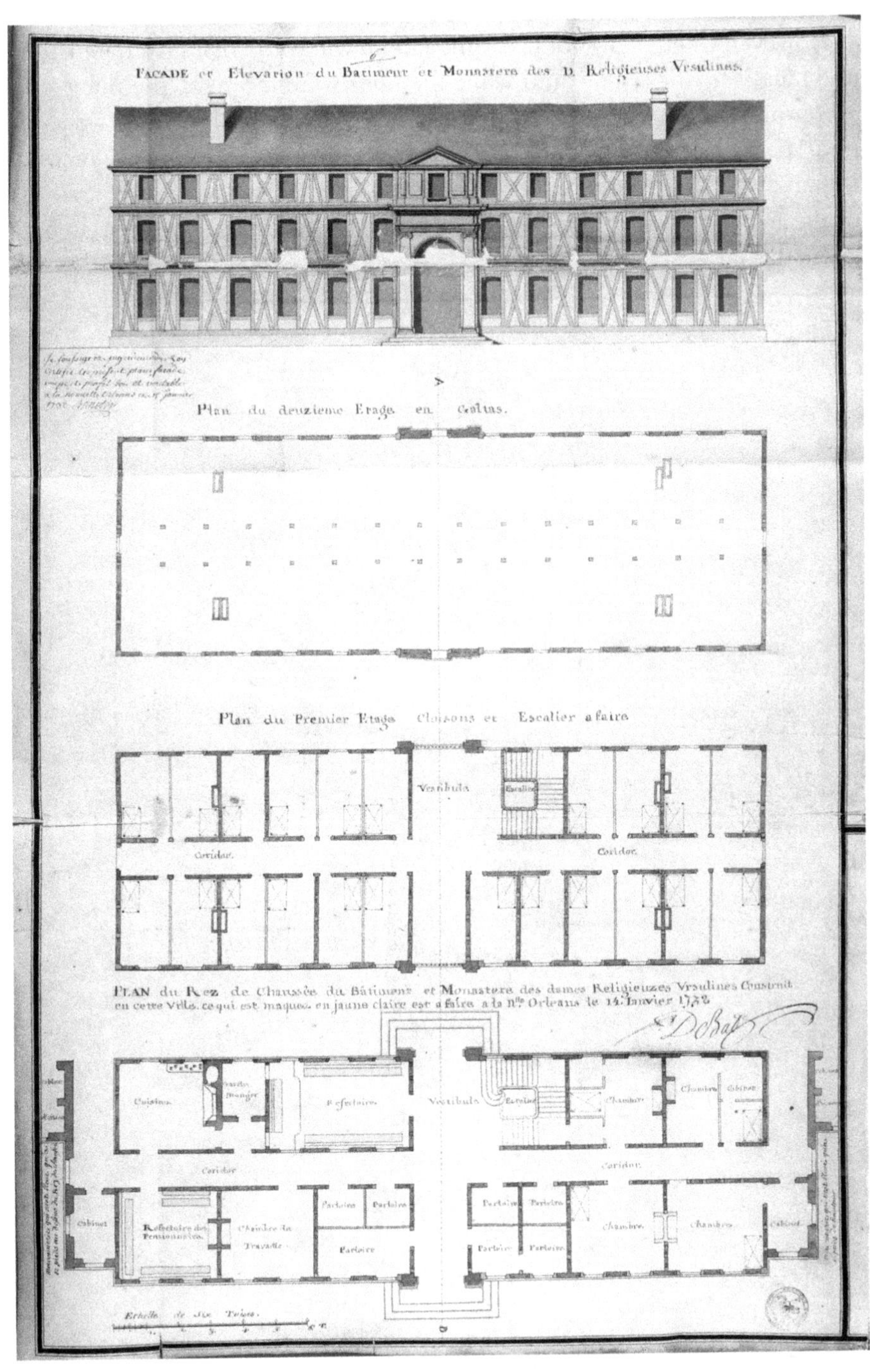

Architectural plans for second Ursuline's Convent. *Courtesy of the Office of Archives and Records Archdiocese of New Orleans.*

However, while many young women, both white and black, were nurtured and taught by the sisters, and while the nuns were aware of the many girls sent from France to New Orleans, it seems the Casket Girls never crossed the nuns' path. Nor had the nuns seen any of the celebrated John Law recruits. In her letters to her father, Sister Hachard writes, "One cannot see at all any of the girls that were said to have been sent here by force. None seem to have come this far."

3
The Business of the Attic

The first convent for the Ursulines, a three-story structure, was completed in 1734. The edifice was of wood frame construction and filled with brick in a somewhat archaic fashion, even for that time. The structure did not fare well in the southern elements. The nuns almost immediately reported the building's faults.

After much negotiation and financial compromise, a new, smaller two-story structure, with an attic instead of a third floor, was constructed, under the plans drawn by the king's engineer, Ignace Broutin, who had also designed the first structure. It wasn't until 1752 that it was completed and approved. This structure is one of the oldest in the Mississippi Valley and is the only original French Colonial structure that survived the devastating French Quarter fires of 1788 and 1794.

In the legend, the Ursuline nuns held hostage the maidens who had been turned vampire during their journey to New Orleans on the ship *La Baleine*, which sailed in 1721. However, the Ursulines did not arrive in New Orleans until the much later date of 1728, and they did not occupy the convent until 1734. Taking this into consideration, the Casket Girls would then have been in limbo for some 13 years.

The girls who sailed on *La Baleine* arrived in Biloxi and under the chaperonage of Sister Gertrude were married there. Records show that the girls were married by Father Charles de St. Alexis, and Sister Gertrude acted as witness. However, Sister Gertrude never traveled to New Orleans. She was sent back to France shortly after her charge of ensuring the girls' marriages were accomplished.

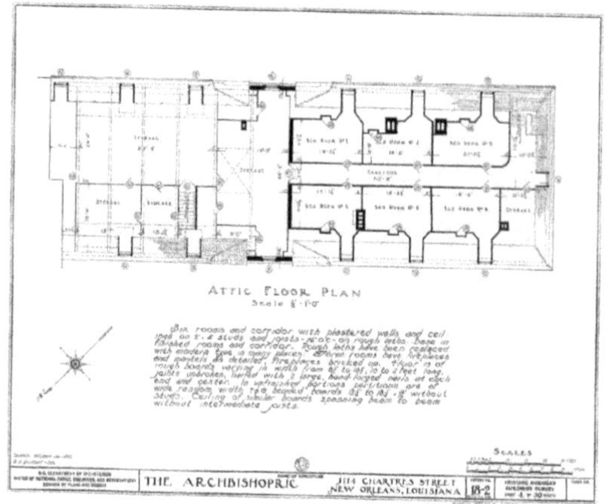

Architectural plans of the Ursuline's Convent attic. *Courtesy of the Office of Archives and Records Archdiocese of New Orleans.*

Yet in the modern book *New Orleans Ghosts, Voodoo and Vampires,* author Kalila Katherine Smith tells of many individuals on her tour, as well as her own experience of walking at night by the convent, and being overwhelmed by the feeling of thousands of peering eyes causing a shiver through their bones. Is this their minds simply engaging them in the fantasy? Or is there something more to the mysterious attic?

In 1819, the city council voted to continue Chartres and Governor Nicholls Streets through part of the nuns' property. This would interrupt both their extensive herb garden, necessary for use in medicinal purposes for the sick they were tending to, as well as intrude on their cloistered privacy. Thus the nuns had a third convent constructed on Dauphine Street that has since been demolished. The nuns gifted the Ursuline convent to the bishop of New Orleans at the time, and over the years, the convent has been remodeled several times, but always under the supervision of the Vieux Carre Commission, a governing office dedicated to maintaining the heritage of the French Quarter. Currently, the building serves as the Catholic Cultural Heritage Center of the Archdiocese of New Orleans.

The attic, however, does have its curiosities. The layout for the attic was designed to house orphans, with six-bed chambers, each with its own dormer window. The remainder of the attic was used for storage. It is described on the U.S. Department of the Interiors plan as having six rooms and a central corridor with plastered walls and ceilings. Three rooms have fireplaces and mantels with the fireplaces bricked up. The floor is described as rough boards varying in width.

Curiously, there is no mention in the plans for one particular room in the attic. As explained by the current convent representatives, this room was set up for individuals under the nuns' care who were suffering from insanity. The floor in this room is all brick, rather than wood, which is featured in the remainder of the attic. It was explained that the brick floor was necessary so that it could easily be washed down from vile acts of the insane. The door to this room is a Dutch door, where plates of food or other items could be handed over quickly and no entrance to the room was necessary, to protect the nuns from any contact with violence.

Today, the attic remains mostly empty, with a little space earmarked as storage for the archdiocese archives. However, every now and then a shutter is forced open through the vicious pounding of a storm. Many have said they have witnessed a face in the window peering out; others have felt eyes watching them through the shutters. It is never long that a shutter stays unlocked. Is this simply because those watching the building take great care in its appearance? Or is there something else at play? Some things one might say are better left to the mystery so that the legend may live on.

This story of the Casket Girls has evoked interest from many individuals over the years, so much so that several fantastical novels have been written with varying angles on the fiction surrounding the story, including *Savage Lands* by Clare Clark, *The Last Casquette Girl* by Lorena Dureau, *The Lost Reflection* by Bruce Jones and *The Casquette Girls* by Alys Arden. The story also inspired Victor Herbot to write an operetta in two acts, first performed in 1910 and the film version was released in 1935 by MGM. The popular contemporary television show *The Originals*, a spinoff of *The Vampire Diaries*, used a version of the story of the Casket Girls in the first season, episode 10. The legend is also featured on many New Orleans vampire tours held throughout the city, and it has been featured on television documentaries such as *Monsters and Mysteries in America*, SWAMP, part 5. The story has so much mysterious flavor, it has been celebrated in all forms of literature and film.

The many errors historians have made in their documentation of the girls from France and their association with the Ursulines helped to manifest what has become a curious and interesting legend.

4

The Casket Girls

The Legend Lives On

Now that all the facts are on the table, why not retell the legend with the facts as a guide? Here is one option of how the legend might be told.

The year was 1721, the time of New Orleans's infancy. A great need for marriageable women to help colonize Louisiana was burdening the governing forces. Thus, twelve young girls were selected from a hospital in France, la Salpêtrière, a boarding facility with a suspicious reputation. It was a home for orphans, prisoners and the mentally insane. Between twelve and seventeen years of age, the girls who were chosen had been raised, many of them from birth, in the walls of la Salpêtrière. While it was not at their discretion whether they would stay in France or embark on the journey to New Orleans, heading toward a questionable future, one might think the chance for any adventure out of the walls of la Salpêtrière would have been a welcome one.

Uncertain of their fate, the girls were put under the chaperonage of Sister Gertude, also of la Salpêtrière. She was said to have ruled with an erratic nature. Her charge was to keep the girls safe on the ship and behind lock and key, during evening hours, so they would not be deflowered. La Salpêtrière was a dark, gruesome place, where historically not just orphans, mentally ill and insane were housed, but also diabolical creatures were rumored to have been held captive there when necessary. In addition to ensuring the Casket Girls had safe passage, the sister, a creature of sorts herself, was to dispose of, while at sea, a very dangerous passenger. The girls traveled with large trousseaus, also referred to as caskets at the time.

Sister Gertrude traveled with a casket of her own, you see. It was the casket of one very dangerous vampire.

Bienville writes of a trick Sister Gertrude, the girls' chaperone, played during the voyage. The sister was clearly jealous of the young maidens and the attention they received, adored by all they met. The sister might just have released that creature in the girls' locked chambers on one evening at sea. Perhaps the sister made a pact with the vampire, whom she was supposed to dispose of. It is rumored that one girl said just before she went dizzy at night that she had seen a small black cat in their chambers. Just thereafter, she was visited by a dark figure who seemed to entrance her, and then mysteriously, she went faint. The girls were all reported to be weak from poor nutrition, but could their weakness have come from the first bite of the vampire? Perhaps night after night, they were being visited by the creature who was slowly turning these girls into prisoners to darkness at Sister Gertrude's direction.

Meanwhile, the girls were kept under lock and key at night. During the day, when others roamed on deck, the girls were now nowhere to be seen. However, the dark sealed quarters of the ship certainly made it possible for nocturnal creatures to be quite safe during daylight hours. Many passengers were hit by illness during the journey, some actually dying. While not thought of as unusual at the time, many now question whether those passengers weren't fated at the hands of something sinister. Could they have been nourishment for the vampire and the maidens who were under its spell?

Sister Gertrude was chagrined, as the girls seemed to become more and more beautiful during the voyage. Once they reached Louisiana, Sister Gertrude was the sole witness as each girl was quickly wed, all by night. However, she was then shipped immediately back to France, quite in her favor, as she avoided any consequences of her actions. It is said that there is no record of these girls ever having made it to New Orleans. However, over the years, there was much illness in the city of New Orleans during these times, and that is the primary reason the Ursulines were sent to the city. It is very likely that once the girls accepted their new existence, they made their way to this city known for its sinister side. It was perfect for a creature of the night. They could feast on the prisoners, prostitutes and vagrants, as who would be missing them?

Sister Mary Hachard, the youngest of the Ursulines, wrote five long letters to her father during her travels to New Orleans, in one of which she makes a point of mentioning, very poignantly, a small cat: "We also took a pretty little cat that wanted to be a part of our community, taking for granted that it could find little mice and rats in Louisiana just as in France."

Well, it is rumored that the king found out about Sister Gertrude's shenanigans during the voyage to Louisiana and now feared for the safety of the people of Louisiana at the hand of the vampire maidens. However, it was agreed that it was no fault of the girls themselves what they had become, so the order was made that Sister Gertrude would sail with the Ursulines under cover. However, Sister Gertrude was never seen on the ship *La Baleine*; there was only a small pretty cat. Sister Gertrude had been given a little rope but had greatly taken advantage of the freedom the king afforded her. Now found out, perhaps her punishment was not to scurry for little mice and rats, but sent to the Ursulines in cat form, the sister was made to travel back to New Orleans and one by one, find and capture the Casket Girls. She was to bring them under the care of the nuns until the convent was built, and there they would be housed under lock and key for eternity, under Sister Gertrude's eternal observation. It was, after all, at her hand that the horror of the girls' fate had transpired.

The Casket Girls would indeed remain in the convent under Sister Gertrude's perpetual patrol. However, the girls would also receive the care of the Ursulines. They would be educated, given love and spiritually nurtured to recapture whatever humanity they were capable of in their current situation. The nuns were driven to help women of all types and certainly those who had been the victims of a cruel, immoral and immortal joke.

The Ursulines were made privy to the vampire maidens once they arrived in New Orleans. The girls were brought one by one to the house on Bienville Street. Sister Gertrude anxiously awaited the convent's security and convenience to its hospital. She was currently forced to hunt daily around town, directing rats to the maidens to feast on for blood that was the necessity for their survival.

Finally, the time came in 1735 that the first convent was built. It was quite a predicament now to get the vampires from the house on Bienville Street to the convent without notice. It was decided that the cloistered nuns, rather than travel quickly in buggies to the convent with caskets in tow, would make a statement of their presence in New Orleans with a procession from the Bienville house to the convent. Their procession, with music and costumes, would drive attention away from the several caskets they traveled with behind the parade, concealed under a canopy.

The vampires were then held captive on the third floor and fed the blood of the ill, which worked for their circumstances. Later, when the convent was rebuilt in 1952, they were only afforded an attic. Some of them had attempted on more than one occasion to escape, so it was decided an attic could be kept more secure. In addition, a special room was built, for protection of the nuns, where the vampires could be punished in seclusion when necessary, until they were once again brought to reason. It is said that occasionally, one of the girls would go mad to the cloister, which was their eternal prison. The nuns were then forced to secure the vampire in this room. It is the only room in the attic with a brick floor, and heavy chains are secured to the beams. There is a double door so that the nuns were not forced to enter the room but could simply toss rats in for the girls to feed on. There in the third-floor attic they stay under the protection of the church and the archdiocese.

Many say that when they wander past the convent at night, they feel eyes peering deep into their souls. These are the eyes of the maidens who were robbed of their humanity and then their freedom at the hands of one sour spinster, Sister Gertrude—centuries of anger, desire, confusion and sadness held captive in one attic. A small cat is said to be seen now and then, roaming the convent ground. Sister Gertrude's curse remains as guardian of the Casket Girls.

Part Two

The Comte St. Germain

5
The Mysterious Gentleman Who Would Not Eat

Late one night in 1903, a woman leaped from the French Quarter balcony of the home of prominent socialite Jacque St. Germain, landing in a very unfortunate situation of great pain and injury among a few late-night stragglers who were just ending their evening. Terrified, she ranted and screamed of having been attacked by a vampire. Bystanders called police to the corner of Royal and Ursuline to investigate the tragic accident. This bizarre tragedy ignites the second legend of vampires in the French Quarter.

Sometime in the early 1900s, a very mysterious man arrived in New Orleans under the name of Jacque St. Germain. Handsome, elegant, wealthy, entertaining, extravagant, mysterious and a bit curious, his reputation both preceded him and continues to live on through the French Quarter vampire tours, where his story and his connection to the unusual event above feature as one of the city's vampire legends.

The eccentric Jacque St. Germain is said to have taken residence at the home located at 1039 Royal Street. St. Germain was apparently a cavalier and quite a ladies' man, frequently seen with a beautiful woman on his arm while strolling through the French Quarter or clubbing in elegant locales late into the night. He delighted in throwing elaborate dinner parties for the city's socialites. His parties were highly anticipated due to their lavish cuisine, fine wine and entertainment. Most relished, however, was his own conversation. St. Germain fascinated his guests with stories of France, Italy, Africa and even Egypt. Visitors were delighted and amused by his eloquent grasp of the English language. They were a bit confused, however, when he

The French Quarter home known as St. Germain's previous residence. *Author's collection.*

spoke of historical occasions hundreds of years in the past with such precise details, as though he had participated in the events themselves. Many of his guests placed little value in the truth of his tales but embraced them for their entertainment value during their visits to his home.

It was not long after his arrival to New Orleans that St. Germain claimed he was a direct descent of the Comte de St. Germain, a close friend and servant of King Louis XV in the eighteenth century. His claim aroused skepticism, but his resemblance to the nobleman was uncanny. Eagle-eyed guests noted that portraits never depicted the Comte as older than forty, the same age that Jacque St. Germain had appeared since he arrived in New Orleans. Rumors started to spread in jest that Jacque St. Germain may, in fact, be the celebrated Comte St. Germain himself, somehow rendered immortal and ageless. Jacque seemed to enjoy the mystery he had created around his persona and neither confirmed nor denied it.

As time went on and his parties became increasingly lavish, gossip of all types began to sprout and circulate around the city, often reaching St. Germain himself, who seemed both entertained and a little satisfied with

Royal Street as it appeared when St. Germain is said to have made it his home. *The Collins C. Diboll Vieux Carre' Digital Survey at the Historic New Orleans Collection, N-568.*

the attention. One of these rumors stemmed from the very curious notion that Jacque never seemed to eat, not even at his own soirees. Moreover, he also had everything catered, down to the fine china, crystal glasses and even silverware. This was especially curious, insomuch as in this time period it was a very recognized and common practice to flaunt one's wealth with fine silver utensils. Spoons particularly were highly decorated, and all utensils were often engraved with the family monogram, to show the wealth of the house. A person of stature, especially one such as St. Germain, who enjoyed entertaining so lavishly, would have had fine silverware. It surely added to his mysterious persona and had everyone wondering what on earth he used on a daily basis—that is, if he ate at all.

As reported on the website of the highly prestigious antique house M.S. Rau,

> *To display just how wealthy you were was of the utmost importance to maintain, if not raise, your standing in high society. These displays took many forms, but it was the dinner party that proved to be an affair that could make or break a socialite. Even the extravagance of the utensils you provided for guests was considered proportionate to one's wealth.*

Left: Comte St. Germain. *Public domain.*

Right: Chest of fine silverware. *Courtesy of M.S. Rau Antiques, New Orleans.*

Not only were St. Germain's parties catered, the host was said to have relished in his guests' satisfaction of the offered feasts without partaking himself, often standing apart from the table drinking from a lavish chalice, presumably filled with wine. During dinner, he offered fantastical recollections of his adventures for his guests' enjoyment. The very strange habit of not partaking in meals at his own soirees, coupled with his remarkable resemblance to the Comte St. Germain, had some in the city suggesting in good fun that perhaps the mysterious man was a vampire.

This brings us to that bizarre evening several months after St. Germain's arrival to New Orleans when the police were called to St. Germain's home to investigate the suspicious situation of the woman who had seemingly fallen from his gallery, a full story above.

His guest, a woman who was rumored to have been a prostitute, had, in fact, jumped from his balcony, rather than fallen, as bystanders had originally surmised. While she survived the fall, she was terrified. People on the street surrounded her and tended to her needs while help was rounded up. Hysterical, the woman ranted that she had purposely jumped to escape St. Germain, who had bitten her neck. She screamed and sobbed out her story, claiming she was only able to escape when her assailant was briefly distracted by a rather loud knocking on his door.

The woman was taken to the hospital as soon as possible, and the police, suspecting that she had become delusional, told the very well-known, affluent and respected St. Germain not to bother coming in for questioning at this late hour, but rather to please visit the police station in the morning to go over the accounts of the evening. The police were confident that there was a reasonable explanation for what had transpired.

The next morning, St. Germain never appeared at the police station. In fact, to everyone's chagrin, he had completely vanished overnight, leaving the majority of his belongings behind.

Legend continues to suggest that upon breaking into his house, the police were cautious and in great anticipation of what they might encounter. On the second floor of the house they discovered a series of open but corked wine bottles. Upon closer investigation, they discovered the large collection of bottles were filled with a terrifying mixture of wine along with good quantities of human blood.

Jacque St. Germain was never seen again. He disappeared just as mysteriously as he had arrived. As one can only imagine, his contemporaries were shocked at this scandal, feeling both betrayed and fooled and probably a little disappointed that the fun had come to an end.

Questions remained unanswered, and this is where the legend of Jacque St. Germain as vampire began to flourish. Had in fact "the" Comte St. Germain of the 1700s made his way to America?

6
The Courtier

Twentieth-century New Orleans socialites noted Jacques St. Germain's resemblance to eighteenth-century nobleman the Comte de St. Germain, and the similarities between the two don't end there. The stories of both St. Germains closely parallel each other, although the elder has a great deal more written material to sink your teeth into. So much mystery, speculation and silliness exist in writings around the Comte's persona that at times, one could almost conclude him a fictional character but for the fact that many affluent leaders and prominent personalities of the time make note of his existence.

A letter from Horace Walpole, the Fourth Earl of Oxford, to his friend Horace Mann provides the first unchallenged reference of St. Germain:

> *An odd man, who goes by the name of Comte St. Germain. He had been here these two years, and will not tell who he is, or whence, but professes that he does not go by his right name. He sings, plays on the violin wonderfully, composes, is mad, and not very sensible. He is called an Italian, a Spaniard, a Pole; a somebody that married a great fortune in Mexico, and ran away with her jewels to Constantinople, a priest, a fiddler, a vast nobleman. The Prince of Wales has had unsatiated curiosity about him, but in vain.*

With no official birth records available, the true origins of the Comte St. Germain are a matter of some disagreement among historians. Prominent nineteenth-century Theosophist (a branch of occultism) Isabel Cooper-

Prince Franz-Leopoid Rakoczy of Transylvania. *Public domain.*

Oakly alludes in her book *The Comte de St. Germain, the Secret of Kings*, that he was most likely born at Lentmeritz in Bohemia at the end of the seventeenth century and is said to have been the youngest son of Prince Franz-Leopold Rakoczy of Transylvania and the Princess Charlotte Amalia of Hesse-Wahnfried. Because of the tumultuous political environment at the time, it is said that as an infant he was placed under the care of the last Medici family, Gian Gastone, which many have speculated may have contributed to his very rich education.

Since that book, many later writers have referenced his beginnings as a Rakoczy as fact. However, in the well-researched work *The Comte De Saint Germain, Last Scion of the House of Rakoczy*, author Jean Overton Fuller confirms that it is only speculation.

St. Germain's refusal to give his true name, except to the King of France, Louis XV, seems to prove that he was, in fact, protecting some house of royalty. While it was common to use many titles in this day and age, it was highly unusual and suspect when asked by a figure of authority to not give up one's true identity. However, the acceptance of his presence so close to the king also indicates that the king was satisfied with his explanation, received in private, of his origins.

Arriving in France in 1756, St. Germain wished to help the French economy with an invention. He was there to present the king with his method of creating vibrant dyes for use in clothing and other materials. His arrival at this time is documented by a letter that seemed to have been penned for him, by most likely a clerk. It is the one and only time he uses what looks like a Christian name. The letter is signed:

> *I have the honour to be…*
> *Denis de S.M.*
> *Comte de St. Germain*

In her book, Fuller writes: "Could he really have been baptized Denis, or is the name of this patron saint of France another hieroglyph, and what is S.M.? We cannot know." Very much like Jacque St. Germain in New Orleans, the Comte St. Germain spun fantastical tales, purportedly claimed to have had conversations with Cleopatra and the Queen of Sheba and professed to have been present during remarkable historical milestones, many of which took place over five hundred years prior.

Cooper-Oakly explains that some of the historical confusion surrounding the Comte's claims stems from his tremendous use of a variety of titles, as was customary at the time, a custom that was tolerated in French society to present that one was not simply a commoner but rather came from some service to the king. From 1720 to 1822, St. Germain was said to have masqueraded under various titles. He had titles that would best suit his needs at the time and add confusion when he was discussed in various circles, both political and social, including:

The Marquis de Montferrat, Comte Bellamarre or Aymar at Venice, Chevalier Schoening at Pisa, Chevalier Weldon at Milan and Leipzig, Comte Sotikoff at Genoa and Leghorn, Graf Tzarogy at Schwalback and Triesdorf, Prinz Ragoczy at Dresden, and Comte de St. Germain at Paris, The Hague, London, and St. Petersburg.

It is very difficult to discern truth from fiction with the Comte's own foolery, coupled with that of writings that came much later.

The Comte de Saint Germain is said to have been an aristocrat with no profession. However, he certainly must have profited from his association with King Louis XV of France, as well as his diplomatic involvement with other political leaders. In fact, it was his ability to produce funds in abundance, whenever necessary, that had him under suspicion of being a spy.

Monsieur Chiquet, French chargé d'affaires in London, said of St. Germain:

I find, also a person who has been here for some time, known here as the Comte de Saint-Germain. He has met every highly placed person, including the Prince of Wales. He speaks several languages, French, English, German, Italian, etc., is a very good musician and plays several instruments, said to be a Sicilian and of great wealth. What has drawn suspicion on him is that he has cut a very fine figure here, receiving great sums and settling all bills with such promptitude that it has never been necessary to remind him. Nobody could imagine how a man who was simply a gentleman could dispose of such vast resources, unless he were employed as a spy. He has been left in his own apartment under the guard of a State Messenger; no papers have been found in it or on his person which furnish the least evidence against him, he has been interrogated by the Secretary of State, to whom he does not furnish an explanation of himself quite so satisfactory as that gentleman wishes, persisting in his refusal to state his real name, title or occupation, unless to the King himself, for, he says, his behavior has been in no wise contrary to the laws of this county, and it is against common right to deprive an honest foreigner of his liberty without formulating an accusation.

It is not known if he did in fact see the king at this time or if he made his case satisfactorily, as not long after being detained, he was indeed released.

Comte St. Germain is said to have been well accomplished in a variety of areas. He was ambidextrous and a great musician, linguist and alchemist. There are countless tales of him precipitating diamonds out of thin air or

Madame du Pompadour. *Public domain.*

changing worthless stones into precious jewels, manipulating metal into gold, finetuning imperfect diamonds into fused masterpieces and creating an elixir of life, which many in his circles at the time felt must have been responsible for his own youthful appearance and health.

He was also in very good company. Author Isabel Cooper-Oakley recounts his having hobnobbed with such prestigious figures as Marie Antoinette, Catherine the Great, Voltaire, Rousseau, Mesmer and Casanova.

While records, including several letters both from the Comte to famous personalities and letters to and from personalities at the time regarding

Right: Boutique du Vampyre, 709½ St. Ann Street. *Author's collection.*

Below: Boutique du Vampyre, interior. *Author's collection.*

Above: Vampire Hunting Kit by artist Deborah Petronio. *Author's collection*.

Left: Traditional monogramed silverware. *Courtesy of M.S. Rau Antiques, New Orleans.*

Advertisement placed in France to promote Louisiana. *The Historic New Orleans Collection, ACC. No. 1952.3.*

Close-up of music book mural open to Aria *Per Pieta' bel idol mio* and dedicated to St. Germain. *Photo by David Wrightson.*

Above: Triangle Book of St. Germain. *Courtesy of the Getty's Open Content Program.*

Left: St. Germain fortune-telling machine. *Author's collection.*

New Orleans Pharmacy Museum, 514 Chartres Street. *Author's collection.*

Urn used to contain leeches, pictured at New Orleans Pharmacy Museum. *Author's collection.*

French Quarter barber's pole, at the Monteleone barbershop, 625 Bienville Street. *Author's collection.*

St. Louis Cathedral, Jackson Square. *Author's collection.*

Pirate's Alley Café, 622 Pirate's Alley. *Author's collection.*

Interior, Toulouse Dive Bar, 730 Toulouse Street. *Author's collection.*

Mysterious bookcase in the Toulouse Dive Bar. *Author's collection.*

Left: Entrance to the Dungeon nightclub, 738 Toulouse Street. *Author's collection.*

Below: Lafitte's Blacksmith Shop bar, 941 Bourbon Street. *Public domain.*

Left: Interior of Potions, French Quarter magical speakeasy. *Author's collection.*

Below: Potions signature cocktail, Potions' Poison, champagne with red absinthe. *Author's collection.*

Left: Eerie stairwell inside Muriel's restaurant, leading to the Séance Rooms. *Author's collection.*

Middle: Muriel's wine room dining table. *Author's collection.*

Bottom: Muriel's Séance Rooms, 801 Chartres. *Author's collection.*

New Orleans street at night.
Author's collection.

Vaults in St. Louis No. One Cemetery. *Author's collection.*

Left: Family tomb, located in St. Louis No. One Cemetery. *Author's collection.*

Below: Tomb of Marie Laveau, the voodoo Queen of New Orleans. *Author's collection.*

Jesus statue in St. Anthony's Garden, located behind the St. Louis Cathedral. *Author's collection.*

Inside Anne Rice Vampire Lestat Fan Club Ball. *Photo by Becky Plexco.*

This page: Costumed guests at an Anne Rice Vampire Lestat Fan Club Ball. *Photos by Becky Plexco.*

Left: Anne Rice, accepting flowers at a ball, pictured with Arianne Swearingen and her mother, Mary Dugas, dressed as Claudia and Madeleine from *Interview with the Vampire*, and Suzie Quiroz, president of the fan club. *Photo by Becky Plexco.*

Below: Statues from Anne Rice's *Queen of the Damned*, at an Anne Rice Vampire Lestat Fan Club Ball. *Photo by Becky Plexco.*

the Comte, confirm that St. Germain did indeed have relations with the aforementioned infamous personalities, still, various documents note that many were not convinced by his eccentricities and charm. Some found him to be an imposter and others a magician of sorts. Casanova was said to have considered him a charlatan, using his charm to coax funds for his elaborate existence. Voltaire is said to have found him long winded, yet entertaining.

Madame de Pompadour was a great fan of Comte de St. Germain. As chief mistress of Louis XV, she had much contact with the Comte and ached for his elixir of life, which he was said to have at some point bestowed on her. According to author Jean Overton Fuller, she is said to have vocalized the following quote in regard to St. Germain:

> *A thorough knowledge of all languages, ancient and modern, a prodigious memoir erudition, of which glimpses could be caught between the caprices of this conversation, which was always amusing and occasionally very engaging, an inexhaustible skill in varying the tone and subjects of his converse; in being always fresh and in infusing the unexpected into the most trivial discourses made him a superb talker. Sometimes he recounted anecdotes of the court of the Valois or of princes still more remote, with much precise accuracy in every detail as almost to create the illusion that he had been an eyewitness to what he narrated. He had traveled the whole world over and the king lent a willing ear to the narratives of his voyages over Asia and Africa, and to his tales about the courts of Russia, Turkey and Austria. He appeared to be more intimately acquainted with the secrets of each court than the charge d'affaires of the king.*

THE MUSICIAN

The next time St. Germain appears in any serious historical document, notes historian Jean Overton Fuller, it is in music. It is said that the Comte St. Germain hid his secrets in musical compositions. "Secrets" most likely meaning secrets of his true existence and his magical accomplishments. Even if that is not true, the following is fantastical enough to make one wonder how this man's genius is at all possible.

In the book *History of Music*, by Charles Burney, the composer of "God Save the King," he writes:

An opera was attempted April 7th, at the little theatre in the Hay-market, under the direction of Geminiani. Prince Lobkowitz, who was at this time in London and fond of music, and the celebrated and mysterious Count Saint-Germain attended all the rehearsals. The opera was a pasticcio, and called L'Incostanza Delusa. But Count Saint-Germain composed several new songs, particularly Per Pieta' bel idol mio, which was sung by Frasi, first woman, and encored every night.

How was a man of such mysterious opportunities given this opportunity to have his original musical compositions performed, and where did he learn his craft? Perhaps he studied music under the care of the Medici family, if in fact that portion of his history is true.

Johann Jakob Heidegger, the manager of the King's Theater from 1713 to 1734, purchased a very famous elaborate home, "4 Maids of Honour Row," upon his retirement in 1744. A scene painter of the King's Theatre painted several murals in the entrance hall, which are remarkably still present to this day. The paintings were Swiss and Italian landscapes, and over the door opening to the stairwell was painted an open book of music, surrounded with a wreath of acanthus, the symbol of immortality. The book, very curiously, was open to *"Per Pieta' bel idol mio,"* the most popular of Saint Germain's arias. Why would so prominent a figure have that particular music featured on his walls, when the piece had not even been performed at the theater? It was performed at a very small opera house that was the King's Theatre's competition. (See insert for a detailed close-up of the mural.)

Like his much later doppelganger, when asked to dinner, Comte de St. Germain's behavior was eccentric, as explained by P. Manly Hall in his introduction to *The Most Holy Trinosophia*: "Frequently invited to dinner, he devoted the time during which he naturally should have eaten to regaling the other guests with tales of magic and sorcery, unbelievable adventures in remote places and intimate episodes from the lives of the great."

The memoirs of the pretended magician and Italian adventurer Giacomo Casanova second this account of the Comte de Saint Germain's curious habit. He writes of how, while dining with Madame la Marquiese d'Urfe', he found that his fellow guest, the Comte de Saint Germain, "did not eat but talked of many branches of science and marvelous things all through the meal."

A possible explanation for why the Comte St. Germain and Jacque St. Germain never seemed to engage in dining among others could simply be that the Comte refused to indulge in the lavish meals he provided for his guests. Some reports specify that he had a very sensible diet, which may have contributed to his fit appearance throughout his existence. A man such as St. Germain, however, surely would have flaunted elaborate silver utensils. As much as he enjoyed entertaining and making sure his means were well known, a man such as this would have had the largest, most elaborate silver spoons and monogramed utensils available at the time. However, Jean Fuller mentions that he was only frank with the king concerning his real name. Perhaps because the Comte went by so many names, he did not find it frugal to monogram or own his own collection. It may have seemed foolish to him to monogram an alias on something as valuable and important as silver, and using non-monogrammed versions may have been suspicious in his circle at the time.

THE ALCHEMIST

Although the Comte could be entertaining and charming, he also demanded respect in his diplomatic dealings. He wrote a letter to the king around 1758 in which he requested accommodations for himself, his staff of Germans and space to work on his most intriguing inventions, seemingly of dyes. He offered the use of the dyes in return to the king, as a means by which to help build the suffering French economy.

One of the most fantastical stories of St. Germain's accomplishments, fixing faulted diamonds, may have been very possible for him at the time. His knowledge of dyes and the dying process was vast and innovative, and most likely he was able to translate it to repairing jewels.

Jean Overton Fuller took it upon herself to contact Messrs De Beers Consolidated Diamond Mines Ltd., posing the question of the possibility of repairing flaws in diamonds. Following is the response she was granted:

> *Improving the colour of a diamond has been practiced for some considerable years. The technique today is to take a badly coloured stone, i.e. a non-descript brown or yellow, and turn it into a rare fancy colour by irradiation. This is bombarding the stone with electrons or neurons. . . . Flawed diamonds could be improved, if the flaw was accessible via a hairline crack in the stone, by boiling in strong acids. This technique is still used today to remove oxidization impurities. These are usually streaks of red, yellow or orange which could be removed or reduced by acids.*

The most notable of accounts in this matter was a request from the king, who possessed a diamond that had been appraised at 6,000 livres. Without a fault it should have captured no less than 10,000. St. Germain took the stone and went to work. A few weeks later, he brought the stone back without a flaw. Upon examination, it was determined to be the same stone. From the same jeweler, he was then presented 9,600 livres for it. However, the king sent the money back, deciding to keep the stone as a curious souvenir.

Rather than magic, possibly St. Germain's innovative techniques translated to the new discoveries he had brought to France.

Karl Heinrich Baron von Gleichen, a guest of the court, met St. Germain sometime in 1759 and was shortly thereafter invited to St. Germain's home for his interest in fine paintings. While von Gleichen was a known exaggerator and romantic and one would be at fault to not sift fact from fiction in his remarks, as explained in historian Jean Overton Fuller's book, he said of St. Germain after the visit to his home:

> *Indeed, he kept his word, for the paintings he showed me were characterized by some singularity of perfection, which made them more interesting than paintings in the first class, above all a Holy Family by Murillo, equal in beauty to the one by Raphael at Versailles but he showed me something else, a quantity of precious stones, mainly diamonds, of surprising size and perfection.*
>
> *I thought I was seeing the treasures of the wonderful lamp. There were amongst them, an opal of monstrous size, a white sapphire the size of an egg, which in its brilliance effaced all stones offered it for comparison. I can dare to say that I know something of stones, and I can assert that the eye could discover no reason to doubt them. They were the easier to inspect as they were not mounted.*
>
> *I stayed until midnight, and when I left it was as his faithful servitor.... I followed him for six months, with the most humble assiduity...*
>
> *While not all the fables and anecdotes relating to the age of Saint Germain merit the attention of serious people, it is true that the collection I have made of testimonies of persons of good faith, who have attested to the long duration and almost incredible preservation of his person, has in it something of the marvelous. I have heard Rameau (Jean-Phillippe Rameau, the composer) and an elderly relative of a French Ambassador to Venice affirm having known Saint-Germain there in 1710, looking like a man of fifty, and Monsieur Morin, who has since then been my secretary at the Embassy, for whose veracity I can speak, told me that he knew Saint-*

King Louis XV of France. *Public domain.*

Germain in Holland in 1735, and was prodigiously astonished at finding him, now, not aged by so much as a year…

He possessed chemical secrets, for the making of colours, dyes and a similor of rare beauty; perhaps he made the stones of which I have spoken, the authenticity of which could only be disproved by a file. But I never heard him speak of a universal medicine.

He kept a very strict regime, never drinking while eating, purging himself with senapods, which he prepared himself, and that was all he had to recommend to those who asked him what they should do to prolong their lives.

The Poet

While there is no evidence of St. Germain having published any poetry of his own, there is much reference of him having been a poet and several poems credited as his work. Jean Overton Fuller mentions the work *The Mystery*, translated to English from the French. St. Germain most likely recited verses in private gatherings, which were later complied into small collections in print such as *Poemes Philosohiques sur l'Homme*, published in Paris by Mercier in 1975. A collection of three poems, *The Mystery* is credited to "le fameux Comte de Saint-Germain":

THE MYSTERY

Scrutator, curious of nature's whole,
I have seen the principle and end of all.
Gold in its puissance, deep in its mine;
I have seized its matter, surprised its leaven.

I can explain the art by which the soul
Within a mother's womb builds house, how swell
Beneath the humid dust pip against grain,
Wheat-ears and vine, bread and wine.

Nothing was; god willed: something became.
The universe rests on what? I stripped
Its frame; nothing bears it. With praise and blame
I weighed the eternal, and it called my soul.
I did, was again god, doubted myself, worshipped.
My cadaver fell. I know no more at all.

Fuller explains that in secret societies, such as Masonry, during the initiation, the new member is figuratively asked to die, so that the soul's spirit is free to see. The all-seeing eye makes reference to a third eye, the eye of the soul. Manly Palmer Hall, a twentieth-century mystic, refers to the very important initiation as outward symbols of inward processes. Perhaps St. Germain is suggesting here that he had been spiritually reincarnated.

THE AUTHOR

There are two books that St. Germain is thought to have authored. The first was procured by the Bibliotheque du Troyes, in France: *La tre's-sainte-Trinosophia* (The most-holy Trinosophia).

There is a note on the first page that reads as follows:

> *This unique manuscript is that which belonged to the famous Cagliostro, and was found by Massena in Rome at the Grand Inquisitor's, and a stuck on note, printed, signed "Philotaume", declared it was the sole existing copy of a work by Saint-Germain.*

Manly P. Hall translated the work and wrote a complex introduction, publishing the work as *The Most Holy Trinosophia* in 1933. It's doubtful that Saint Germain is the true author of the original book, however. Within the work, which details numerous alchemical and magical processes, the author writes of his torturous time as a captive. St. Germain was never imprisoned during the Inquisition. Fuller speculates that it was more likely written by Cagliostro during his capture in the Castel Saint Angelo in the late 1700s.

The other book, held in the Getty Research Center in Los Angeles, is known as the Triangle Book. It is thought that there was more than one, handwritten, each slightly different, so that if not all were presented together, the true secrets within could not be revealed.

The book offers the notion that by following instructions the reader will obtain three ends: "The discovery of all treasure lost at sea; the discovery of diamond, gold and silver mines; and the prolongation of life to a century or over with the freshness and vigor of the age of 50."

A digital copy can be found on the Getty Research website. (See additional photo in insert.)

This most unusual book, circa 1750, was procured from the library of Lionel Hausser, Ancien member du Counseil de Direction de la Societe Theosophique du France. It was sold by Sotheby's Auction House in

London by Manly P. Hall. Much of his occult manuscript collection was later purchased by the Getty Center in Los Angeles.

As described on her website in 2015 by Iona Miller, a self-proclaimed alchemist:

> *The document is of triangular shape, on vellum, and written in cipher with the exception of the title page. The cipher itself is quite simple, belonging to the class found in Masonic documents, and decodes into French. It is titled The Sacred Magic Reveled to Moses, recovered in an Egyptian monument and carefully preserved in Asia under the Device of Winged Dragon. On the first page are the words: "By the gift of the most wise Comte de St. Germain who passed through the circle (center) of the earth". The writing itself belongs to a class known as Grimoire or Manuals of Ceremonial Magic.*

The pages are beautiful and best followed with the illustrations accompanying the text. Miller further writes:

> *The balance of the manuscript is devoted to the consecration of magical implements and prayers to spirits. Most of the formulas are magical rather than alchemical and so involved in obscure symbolism and cabalistic names as to be impractical to the modern reader.*

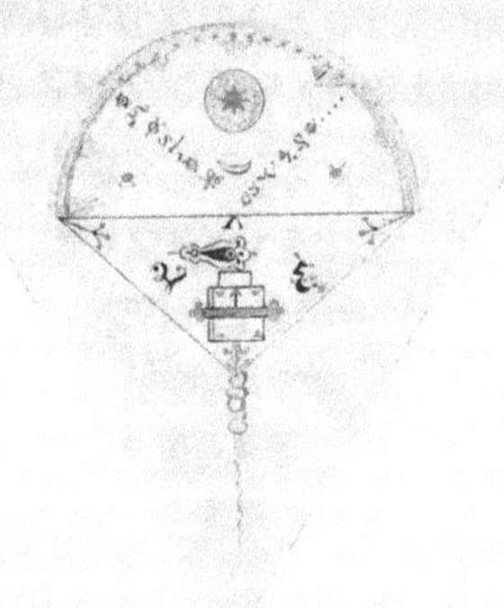

Page from the Triangle Book of St. Germain. *Courtesy of the Getty's Open Content Program.*

> *It is unclear in both cases whether the Comte St. Germain wrote these magical formulas or owned a copy of an ancient text. This manuscript was made for Antoine Louis Moret, a French Émigré to America active in Masonry and in politics.*

The key to the cypher is an accompanying bound volume and was provided with the lot at purchase from the auction house, and is also in the Getty Museum.

In the book are very cryptic messages with fantastic tales that are illustrated with Egyptian hieroglyphs and Masonic symbols. The book ends with:

> *In the name of the Eternal my God, true master of my body, my soul, and my spirt, go, go in peace; retire that you may accompany me always, and be ever ready to come when I shall call you.*
>
> *Amen and Amen.*
>
> *Finis.*

Curiously enough, author Jean Overton Fuller's very detailed account of Comte St. Germain made no mention of the Triangle book. However, she does mention *The Mahatma Letters*, written by Madame Blavatsky's two teachers Morya and Koot Hoomi. Madame Blavatsky was a Russian spirit medium and occultist. *The Mahatma Letters* are an in-depth and precise philosophy and a prophecy concerning a procedure scientists would come to adopt and implement in the twentieth century. A complete transcript of *The Mahatma Letters* can be found at the Theosophical University Press Online Edition, www:theosociety.org/pasadena/mahatma.

Fuller mentions that Koot Hoomi writes in one of these letters, "Saint Germain recorded the good doctrine in the figures and his only ciphered MS remained with his staunch friend and patron the benevolent German Prince from whose house…he made his last exit—HOME. Failure, dead failure!"

Koot Hoomi may be suggesting here that St. Germain's failure lies in his faith that he would be able to enlighten people. However, he did not account for the shortsightedness of so many whom he hoped to touch. It is possible that the mention of the ciphered MS is referring to a note with some sort of instructions which Saint Germain had promised Prince Carl von Hesse, before his "death." However, the prince claimed he never found these notes.

The Master Rakoczy

St. Germain as Ascended Master

For those delving deeper into research, you will undoubtedly come across the work of Mark and Elizabeth Prophet, mid-twentieth-century spiritualists who were under the deep belief that St. Germain was speaking through them as an ascended master. Ascended masters are believed to be spiritually enlightened beings who in past incarnations were ordinary humans but who have undergone a series of spiritual transformations called initiations. The ascended master is based on the Theosophical concept that explores divine wisdom, created by the Theosophical Society, founded in New York City in 1875 by Helena Blavatsky, William Quan Judge and Henry Steel Olcott.

In 1958, Mark L. Prophet founded the Summit Lighthouse, a church of New Age spirituality. Five years later he was joined by his new wife, Elizabeth Clare Prophet, author of the "I Am" discourses, *Saint Germain, Master Alchemist*, *Saint Germain on Alchemy* and several others.

The books are written in chapters/lessons signed by St. Germain and discuss in great length "precipitation"—creating something solid out of nothing more than invisible molecules—much as that which St. Germain was rumored to have accomplished, such as creating diamonds out of thin air. However, they were written by Elizabeth Prophet, who claimed that St. Germain spoke through her.

It seems credit to St. Germain's true accomplishments were overlooked by the Prophets. Rather, they looked to the spirits for godly guidance in fantastical things. They did not see the brilliance in St. Germain, the man, a man who was vastly accomplished, a scientist who figured out elements of the universe way before his time. The Prophets credited St. Germain's accomplishments to spiritualism and supernatural causes rather than to his scientific brilliance.

Elizabeth, upon her husband, Mark's, death on February 26, 1973, assumed control of the Summit Lighthouse. Then in 1975, she founded the Church Universal and Triumphant, which became the umbrella organization for her expanded worldwide movement. Prophet handed day-to-day operational control of her organization to a president and board of directors, maintaining her role as spiritual leader until her retirement due to health reasons in 1999. She passed away on October 15, 2009; however, the church is still following the Prophets' vision today.

7

The "Death" of St. Germain

There are conflicting thoughts surrounding the death of the Comte St. Germain. Fuller gives an abundance of information in her book to St. Germain's end; however even this well-researched account has curious findings.

St. Germain is reported to have passed on February 27, 1784. The Nikolakirche church register, in Eckernförde, reads: "Deceased Febraury 27, 1784, buried on March 2, 1784, the so-called Comte de Saint-Germain and Weldon—further information not known—privately deposited in this church."

Fuller, who is sadly also now deceased, wrote to the town hall of Eckernförde in 1979 regarding the extent of St. Germain's estate. She translates from the German response:

> *I found, in 1925, the deceased's estate act of Saint-Germain.*
>
> *So poor was the Comte that the estate did not cover the cost of his burial. He was given free burial out of regard for his Patron; in the Church itself the adventurer found his peace. Poor he was indeed by the time he lived in Schlewig, for there was found belonging to him only one box, and few things in it.*
>
> *The Landgraf Prince Carl of Hesse took back all his own letters, and personally put in order all papers which he left. He had therefore, the possibility of finding any unknown letters from and to the Comte de Saint-Germain.*

His friend the Prince of Hesse was to visit him, but it is said that St. Germain passed before the prince could make the trip. St. Germain had promised his friend an "MS, notes for instructions on how to proceed." What exactly "proceed" means, we will never know. However, after searching, Prince Carl was not able to find the notes. Because of his stature, St. Germain's effects were gone through with a fine-tooth comb, very possibly for the hope of finding diamonds and other fine jewels. Fuller gives a detailed list of actual belongs left behind by St. Germain, made by the state secretary of Eckernförde, J. Claussen.

It seems that, contrary to his luxurious lifestyle, he must have dispersed of all his wealth before his death, for there was only one box of very simple items of necessity. While the exact items are listed in Fuller's book, it suffices to say the belongings were mostly clothing and toiletries. Perhaps the Comte made peace with dying and had no further use for earthly possessions. Or perhaps he was ready to disappear again and remerge as someone else?

It is reported as being very curious that for a man of his stature, no one of importance was to attend his funeral—almost as if he had not passed away at all. Was it a ruse so that he might continue about his business undetected?

8

St. Germain as Vampire

Perhaps there is only one St. Germain and he has lived across centuries, ageless, with no need for nourishment but the curious mix of wine and human blood discovered in his rapidly abandoned house in New Orleans.

In *The Most Holy Trinosophia* introduction, P. Manly Hall writes: "In one of his tales concerning vampires, St. Germain mentioned in an offhanded way that he possessed the wand or staff with which Moses brought water from the rock, adding that it had been presented to him at Babylon during the reign of Cyrus the Great."

Certainly much that is written of the accounts of St. Germain should be taken with a grain of salt. However, perhaps he did make his way to New Orleans at a time of unrest. It is said that now and then there is an ascended master who is placed here by God to intervene when intervention is necessary for the greater good. Perhaps St. Germain is such a man.

In the time of the 1730s, there are many records on file at the Historic New Orleans Collection of a man by the name of St. Germain, who was an accomplished property owner who also went by the name of Louis Mechin. There are no records of a St. Germain having owned the property at 1039 Royal Street. It is possible, however, that such an adventurer, with the necessity to move about at a moment's notice, may have simply rented the property for his purposes.

While the Comte St. Germain was certainly a unique individual, highly worthy of investigation and research, whether he ever made it to New

Orleans to entertain the socialites of the French Quarter will forever be a mystery.

Today, in the French Quarter, St. Germain can be visited at Boutique du Vampyre in the form of a fortune-telling machine. Safely behind glass, he is there as your spiritual guide. (See insert.)

For those unfamiliar with Comte St. Germain, it is important to note that he is not to be confused with the Bishop of St. Germain (496–576 CE) of Paris, for whom the St. Germain Abby in Paris is named, as well as the forest St. Germain.

Part Three

The Carter Brothers

9

Blood Brothers

The year is 1932. A young girl storms down Royal Street, visibly panicked, her stride broken only by the diligent interception of a police officer. Her story sounds a bit farfetched: tied up by two brothers, along with several other victims, and held captive so the brothers could drink their blood. She claims that she was only able to escape due to her captors' carelessness in securing her ropes. Somewhat skeptical, the police agree to follow her back to the home on the corner of Royal and St. Ann. This is where our third legend of vampires in New Orleans begins.

Once the police and the girl arrived at the Carter brothers' home, they were horrified to find, as the girl had described, four other victims, half dead, tied to chairs in one of the rooms. All victims had their wrists wrapped with bandages, moist and stained with blood. Two more bodies wrapped in blankets were tucked away in yet another room. The unmistakable suffocating odor of death permeated the apartment.

It seemed the brothers left early each morning just before daybreak and returned every evening just after dark. Immediately upon their return, they would take the bandages off each of the captive's wrists and, using a knife, reopen their wounds until blood flowed freely from the victims' cuts. They caught the blood in cups from which they drank until their hunger was sated. The brothers would then redress the wounds with fresh bandages. They spoke very little and gave no concern for their victims' well-being. Rather, the kidnapped were no more than a food source headed for certain death.

The French Quarter property supposed to have been the Carter brothers' residence. *The Collins C. Diboll Vieux Carre' Digital Survey at the Historic New Orleans Collection, VCS -124.*

Unaware that the girl had escaped, John and Wayne Carter went about their routine as usual. Only this time, the police waited for the brothers to return. They were quickly apprehended, and upon their capture, confessed almost immediately, begging to be murdered. The brothers explained to authorities that they were, in fact, vampires and would, if released, have no option but to continue to kill, as their need for drinking blood was beyond their control. It's said the brothers were tried as serial killers, convicted and eventually executed.

How was it that the brothers, thinking themselves vampires, gifted with eternal life, could be so careless in their plans for survival? Perhaps it was the drastic changing environment in New Orleans that ultimately led to their demise.

During the early 1900s and Roaring Twenties, the city of New Orleans was bustling and booming. The busiest port in the country brought flourishing business and plenty of jobs. In fact, the city was coined "The Big Easy" because at the time, work in New Orleans was so easy to find. A surplus of disposable income triggered a new sense of freedom with the celebration of nightclubs, new energetic music called jazz, loose women, the Storyville district and an excitement that was unmeasurable to anything the city had ever seen. It was a time of "anything goes," footloose and fancy free, that also created carelessness among residents and visitors to the city. No one was thinking of danger. If vampires truly had been in New Orleans at the time, it would surely have been easy to feast.

However, just a decade later came the stock market crash and with it the Great Depression. Everything changed almost overnight. People stayed at home, kept to themselves. The only wanderers were derelicts who roamed the city in search of a little easy work for something to eat. The downtrodden could often be found begging for food at back doors of the homes of fine citizens for a little yard work. More often than not, these vagrants were granted work and a plate of food but were never invited into the home. Rather they sat with their plates on the porch steps, thankful for every morsel.

The rug had been pulled out from underneath what had been a flourishing city, and lifestyles changed dramatically. New Orleans, however, known for its southern hospitality, has always found the most heartfelt way to care for its people. Dr. Peter Carl Graffagnion, a student at the time, reflects on the 1930s in his journal. He gives a lovely description of the environment in New Orleans for a youngster on a budget headed for medical school. It seems that seeking out the affordable meal in depressed New Orleans was part of the adventure:

> *Meanwhile, in spite of its prolonged poverty and political troubles, New Orleans in the 1930s was an interesting and enjoyable place in which to spend the student years. The living was easy. Food was cheap; a "poor-boy" sandwich (a half loaf of French bread sliced longitudinally, spread with mayonnaise, and packed with hot roast beef and fixings) cost 25 cents; a five or six course lunch at Maylie's or Tujague's was 50 cents; and in the lake front spots at West End near Bucktown you could eat your fill of boiled shrimp or crabs or crawfish for almost nothing and wash them down with a nickel glass of beer.*
>
> *The French Quarter then, even though subdued and at one of its low ebbs, was probably at its best from a student viewpoint. The droves of today's investing tourists were nowhere to be seen; the handful of drug addicts and reefer-smokers kept to themselves and stayed hidden; there was only an occasional honky-tonk or second-rate night club along all of Bourbon Street, and you could wander around the whole Quarter in complete safety and innocence and never find trouble unless you deliberately set out to seek it.*

Tujague's Restaurant. *Author's collection.*

Today, one can still find the charm in simple, delicious meals when on a budget or simply desiring a little New Orleans tradition. Complimentary red beans and rice can be found on Mondays, also known as washday, in ample supply in several historical restaurants and in many nightclubs through the city. Traditionally, women would put on a pot of red beans in the morning before they started the weekly laundry and, when the laundry was done, so were the rice and beans. Plate specials and private suppers are frequently hosted by families asking under ten dollars a plate for a healthy portion, and daily specials all throughout the city for traditional New Orleans cuisine are plentiful, even in modern-day New Orleans. For a vampire, New Orleans, when it comes to acquiring adequate nutrition, would have changed just as much as it did for mortals.

In the 1930s, for a vampire, stalking vagabonds would likely have been the most reliable source of food. If the Carter brothers and vampires existed in 1930s New Orleans, it would most likely have been the environment of the city at that time that would have led to their mistake. The time of feeding on prostitutes and carefree dock workers was long gone. It was a depressed time, so feeding on the misfortune of derelicts who had nowhere to turn but to the invitation of a vampire was their peril. It is possible that a young girl may have witnessed the capture of such a derelict and the Carter brothers had no choice but to take the youngster hostage as well. One would hope that it was a fluke that such a young victim was reportedly among the brothers' captives, but realistically, what morals do a vampire hold?

10

The Barber Pole

The dramatic change in environment between the Roaring Twenties and the Great Depression must have had some impact on our infamous brothers, as they would have been forced to go from an ample supply to a drastically scarce one. Had the Carter brothers roamed the streets of New Orleans during the high time of the early 1900s and '20s, they would not only have had the very carefree environment to their advantage from which to obtain plentiful food from unsuspecting fun-loving people but also very likely would have found blood at the hands of a curious source. A vampire with a sense of morality, even as late as the 1920s, would have been much behooved to make the good acquaintance of a barber.

As early as 1540 CE, the very early understanding of health and wellness included the idea that bad blood needed to be released from the body, and barbers were the only feasible professionals who could assist in this process at the time. In the Dark Ages, It was even thought that evil came through unkempt hair follicles, and barbers were able to free the soul of evil by trimming hair as short as possible, eliminating the growth of bad intentions. Barbers were called barber surgeons and also engaged in other surgical procedures, such as caring for open wounds, pulling teeth and setting broken bones. Much later, barbers utilized leeches as one means to clean the impurities of contaminated blood from their customers.

Leeches would be kept in ceramic jars or urns in slightly salted water in the pharmacy section of the barbershop. Leeches could be placed almost anywhere on the body. There are even instances where leeches were tied

Carefree New Orleans, 1920s. *Courtesy of the Ralston Crawford Collection, Hogan Jazz Archive, Tulane University.*

to a string to bleed a patient's throat. Once full, the leeches would then be removed, squeezed out and emptied of blood—so that they could quickly be reused. Once the leech was removed, the patient's wound would then be cleaned and wrapped with a bandage. Leeches' saliva contains natural anticoagulant enzymes, which thin the blood of prey, making a bandage necessary to stop bleeding.

There were other means of letting blood at the hands of a barber. The barber would hand the customer a stick to hold tight, which helped expose their veins, and make a clean incision. The blood would be captured in a metal bowl. The hope was that this means of purification would rid the patient of all ailments.

The barber pole, originally just white with a red spiral, was to resemble the red-stained towels blowing in the wind to alert everyone that this was indeed a place where blood could be let. The blue stripe was added much later in the United States, most likely to symbolize American patriotism.

Today, leeches are used for situations in surgery when other means to stop bleeding are difficult to execute. However, the scare of contamination and fear of infections caused by the leeches keep their use to a minimum.

New Orleans was instrumental in the advancement of modern medicine with the first real pharmacy and pharmaceutical license. The pharmacy museum is in this spot today. J. Dufilho Jr. became America's first licensed pharmacist in 1816 after passing a test that was established by the State of Louisiana in 1804. Prior to that, anyone who studied as an apprentice for six months' time could then—without regulation—sell concoctions in any doses they saw fit. As stated on the website of the New Orleans Pharmacy Museum, "Louis J. Dufilho, Jr. was the first to pass the licensing examination, therefore making his pharmacy the first United States apothecary shop to be conducted on the basis of proven adequacy."

Today, the New Orleans Pharmacy Museum, still located where Dufilho's apothecary stood, at 514 Charters Street, displays a wonderful collection of the antiquated remedies used during and prior to 1816. Leeches were only recently removed from the mix. However, it has several tools on display that were used to administer bloodletting, including fleams and scarifiers.

New Orleans Pharmacy Museum. *Author's collection.*

Fleam and scarifier, tools once used for bloodletting. *Author's collection.*

The Carter brothers are believed to have called New Orleans home while Dufilho ran his apothecary, and it is said that they most certainly frequented the spot for quick and trouble-free nutrition, in addition to the handful of barbershops in the city at the time. Many believe that vampires during these times dangled the hope of eternal life as a promise to barbers in return for an ample supply of honest blood—blood that was acquired without harm to any mortal at the hands of a vampire. The promises were usually no more than just that, a promise, as creating another vampire was taken very seriously, and most barbers had no benefit to a vampire unless they were mortal.

Today, with the stylized advancement to men's haircare, there are fewer barbershops, much less ones with barber poles. In the French Quarter, there is such a barbershop at the Hotel Monteleone. Outside, the barber pole alerts customers that it is the kind of place where you can receive an old-fashioned shave and haircut. The owner, Patrick O'Connell, worked at the barbershop when it was featured inside the hotel lobby for many years. As barbershops became less popular, in 1978, the Hotel Monteleone was also eliminating its tonsorial emporium. However, the hotel offered O'Connell the option of converting one of the hotel parking spaces into a small barbershop. He continues to rent this space, which has an old-school feel, and he continues to offer an old-fashioned deal: a shave with a straight razor, complete with hot towel treatment. If you stop in and ask Pat about a barber's relationship with vampires, you may be in for quite a surprise. Pat has had a relationship with Boutique du Vampyre since it arrived in the French Quarter. He may just have some fun facts to share with you.

There was a time when a vampire would have had a much easier time acquiring blood from sources other than taking it from helpless victims. As with so many things, evolution and change takes its toll on the simpler times.

11

A Year and a Day

According to the stories, the police determined that the Carter brothers were mere mortal serial killers, and their deaths were managed accordingly, although no documentation in U.S. death penalty records supports this. At the time of the Carter brothers' legendary crimes, hanging was still the means of execution. The brothers would have been hanged at the then new Criminal Courts building at Tulane Avenue and South Broad Street. Unless they or someone else had made arrangements for a proper burial and purchased a tomb in one of the local cemeteries, their bodies would have been placed in a public vault.

In New Orleans, because of the very swampy earth, caskets have long not been buried under ground. Citizens in the 1700s were horrified when they attempted to bury bodies the traditional way and were greeted with the sight of caskets, loosened from the earth, floating down the streets of New Orleans during storms and floods. They say to this day, when there is flooding and water seeps into the tombs, one can hear the caskets bumping up against the tomb, as if knocking to be let out. So above-ground tombs were put into place to keep the dead secure in their resting places. In New Orleans, bodies are placed in the vaults for one year and one day, at which time they are sure to have completely decomposed. After a year and a day, a ten-foot pole is used to gather any remains, such as ashes and bones, which are then often placed in a burlap bag and pushed to the back of the tomb to make room for another body. This is one possible explanation for where the saying "I wouldn't touch that with a ten-foot pole" actually comes from.

Tomb in St. Louis No. One Cemetery. *Author's collection.*

If you are able to visit the St. Louis No. One Cemetery, located just outside of the French Quarter across Rampart Street, the sinking city is illustrated behind the cemetery walls. There are many vaults of which the bottom row is only marginally visible, as the remainder has over the years sunk beneath the ground. It's chilling to think a city could literally be sinking and swallowed into the ground. They call our cemeteries Cities of the Dead, as the tombs seem to have tales to tell, even if their inhabitants are speechless. Some tombs have housed generations, and when you stand among them, they are more than just cement and rock and marble. One can truly feel the soul of the history they house.

It is unfortunately no longer possible to enter the St. Louis Cemetery unless you are part of a tour, as mischievous vandalism from disrespectful individuals took that right away. That is truly a shame, as walking alone though the rows of the tombs lent itself to an experience like no other. You could almost hear voices whispering to you as you stood dangerously close to a tomb that was over two hundred years your elder. If you find yourself on such a tour, linger back for just a moment and listen.

If the Carter brothers had been Catholic, they would have been placed in one of the group vaults and granted a proper burial, even with their sordid past. There they would have remained a year and a day until their vault was opened to make room for the next unfortunate soul.

However, in regards to the Carter brothers, the legend has it that when their vaults were opened to brush their remains aside, no trace remained of the brothers at all—no bones, no clothes, not a single sign of them.

According to Haunted History Tours, many over the decades have claimed to see two men matching the description of the Carter brothers: tall, thin, proud men, in handsome clothes, one with sideburns and mustache, the other with careless hair, standing on the second-floor balcony of the building on the corner of Royal and St. Ann, peering out over the city and its good, unsuspecting people.

Did the brothers somehow escape their fate and remain to this day to roam the earth, now and then returning to New Orleans?

These are three unique and fascinating legends all spun over centuries in one small neighborhood. Is it the unusual and colorful history the French Quarter has enjoyed since its birth and continues to manifest that ignites the imagination for so many legends to evolve? Perhaps the history of the French Quarter continues to attract those with a liking for exactly that sort of flavor, and these somewhat unusual individuals bring with them more of the same so that new legends may arise.

Part Four

Vampire Evolution over the Centuries

12

Vampire Evolution and Influence on Art and Literature

A very early introduction to the idea of a vampire in literature was from the penny dreadful *Varney the Vampire*. Penny dreadfuls were little pamphlets distributed in England during the depression in the 1800s. While considered trash journalism at the time, these little pamphlets were produced to uplift people's spirits and entice individuals to read. Penny dreadfuls were written of highwaymen and pirates and quickly turned to the gruesome and supernatural to pique readers' interests and keep them engaged. *Sweeny Todd* was a penny dreadful, and then came *Varney the Vampire.*

Varney the Vampire was written by James Malcolm Rymer and Thomas Peckett Prest in 1846–47. Varney is described as a horrifying creature with black metallic eyes, a bloodless face, long nails that literally appear to hang from the fingers and glaring-white fang-like teeth—a creature that would instill terror enough to stop ones' breath. Curt Hurr, in his introductory notes to the modern reprint of *Varney the Vampire*, mentions that Bram Stoker was most definitely influenced by Varney when penning his celebrated *Dracula*; however, Stoker's idea of a vampire was the first to adopt more human-like attributes, contrary to his predecessor. Stoker's adaptation was pivotal in the overall development of the creature. Dracula was able to captivate his victims, controlling their actions with his mind and lulling them into a swoon, drawing them in. Over time, vampires have evolved from disgusting, horrifying creatures to dangerously charismatic and sensual beings.

Another romantic figure that has grown from the vampire creature is the vampire hunter. From Van Helsing to Buffy and Blade, the fiction has

Varney the Vampire, a penny dreadful. *Public domain.*

changed quite a bit. From vampire hunting kits carried in bags or cases similar to a doctors' bag at the time to Blade's elaborate armory, vampire hunters have also evolved through literature. The idea of a historical vampire hunting kit is enticing to anyone. Complete with pistol, stake, Bible, cross and holy water, these kits were supposedly toted around by those on the hunt of a dangerous, bloodthirsty vampire.

Functional vampire hunting kits, genuinely manufactured for use against vampires, are most likely no more than just that, a romantic notion. There have been several kits, marketed as vampire hunting tools, sold at auction houses and antique shops such as Sotheby's and even our local New Orleans antique house, M.S. Rau. The question is, did people over the centuries really take the threat of vampires seriously enough to manufacture actual vampire hunting kits? It is more likely that if an authentic vampire hunting kit exists, it must have been put together by an individual who believed in vampires and thus compiled various tools thought adequate to end the life of a vampire on his own. There is no evidence that any such kits were ever commercially manufactured.

A very detailed article debunking the origin of vampire hunting kits can be found on vamped.org, a website created and maintained by Anthony Hogg and Erin Chapman. Hogg explains that the first time in history when a vampire hunting kit was actually manufactured or assembled was most likely in the late twentieth century, and the idea sparked in media. In his online article "6 Reasons Why You Shouldn't Buy an 'Antique' Vampire Hunting Kit," Anthony Hogg explains:

> *Caveat emptor, indeed. If you want to bid on a "19th century" vampire killing kit, always ask the dealer how they've verified the kit's age. Ask for supporting documentation. If you see one of these things displayed in a museum, ask similar questions. Though it's counter-intuitive, don't presume "19th century" means the kit was manufactured during that era.*

Hogg interviewed several individuals, including Michael Hirsch, the president at Ripley's Believe It or Not!, who claim to have the largest collection of such kits in their possession. No real authentication was ever afforded Hogg during his interviews to support the claims that these kits were manufactured for the precise purpose of killing vampires. Only romantic speculation is at the stem of any truth to these items.

However, while these kits are not necessarily authentic, they are still very valuable. Upon close examination, an authenticator may determine the box, the pistol, knives, crosses and even the Bibles all to have originated within the same period. However, these individual pieces were most likely put together much later to compile the kit. That is what has made it so difficult for people to discern the kits' authenticity.

While vampire hunting kits may never have been produced in a sophisticated, marketable manner, one can still argue that a superstitious "vampire hunter" in the 1800s might have put together his own kit with various items thought to be necessary to end a vampire's existence. The truth in that would be almost impossible to prove or disprove. Regardless, the notion of vampire hunting kits has become a very romantic one over the years.

See the color insert for a photo of a vampire hunting kit, created as a piece of artwork in a class by Michael DeMeng, an artist who brings a creative conference to New Orleans annually, wherein the attendees create a themed piece of artwork during each session. One year, the theme happened to be vampire hunting kits. This particular kit was created by artist Deborah Petronio and is only one of many remarkable pieces that were created for the class by various artists in 2014.

13
SANGUINARIAN

From what originated as horrific creatures that were truly terrifying, such as the creature Count Orlok in the 1922 horror film *Nosferatu*, to a more sophisticated version in Bram Stoker's *Dracula*, to the sexy, romantic versions portrayed today in shows like *True Blood* and films like *Twilight*, vampires have evolved tremendously.

The mere word *vampire* connotes romantic, exciting, enticing images, such as the elaborate vampire hunting kits recreated to ensnare the imagination. The costumes and jewelry and makeup that are associated with the image of a vampire have become magical and not nearly as terrifying as they once were.

With this in mind, one can look at evolution for a vampire as pleasing, as it puts them in a much more accepting light, probably making it easier for them to mix and once again obtain their blood by means more suitable to today's environment. In fact, there are vampire lifestylers, some of which are referred to as Sanguinarian, who are involved in drinking human blood. The word *sanguine* refers to blood. A wonderful definition is offered by Vocabulary.com:

> Sanguine *is from Latin* sanguis *"blood" and originally meant "bloody"—in medieval medicine it described someone whose ruddy complexion was a sign of an optimistic outlook. That was back when people thought that "bodily humors" like blood were responsible for your attitudes. Now that we no longer believe in humors,* sanguine *has settled down as*

Actor Friedrich Gustav Maximillian "Max" Schreck as vampire Count Orlok in *Nosferatu*, 1922. *Public domain.*

> *a fancy way to say someone is cheerfully confident. Experts are frequently described as feeling sanguine about a political or economic situation—or not sanguine, if they think we're going to hell in a handbasket.*

These "vampire lifestylers" have relationships with donors who freely offer their blood to them. Some say they feel they need the blood, while others do this ritual to feel more connected to vampires. In October 2015, Yanan Wang wrote an article titled "Inside the Human Blood-Drinking, 'Real Vampire' Community of New Orleans," following John Edgar Browning, a former doctoral candidate at Louisiana State University, in his quest for meeting real blood-drinking vampires. Browning learned that people become donors for various reasons; some are close friends of those claiming to need blood and others give their blood for financial reasons and some for sexual favors. In a study reported by the Atlanta Vampire Alliance, there are at least five thousand individuals who identify as vampires in the United States, fifty of whom reside in New Orleans. Either way, the evolution of what vampires have become—glamorous yet dangerous—has once again opened avenues for real vampires to acquire blood through more acceptable means.

New Orleans is probably the best place for individuals craving a vampire lifestyle. New Orleans vampire tour guides are able to walk through the French Quarter in full vampire attire, fangs in place, and instead of being judged by people engaged in more average walks of life, they are treated as rock stars. In fact, they are able to use their style to secure good work, where tourists hang on their every word, as they walk groups through the Quarter in the dark, telling vampire legends. Often people on the tours wonder for just a moment if their tour guide could be a vampire. It's a wonderful dynamic for this handful of individuals, allowing them to shine instead of suppressing their desires.

If a tour guide is not your bag, there are other options here in the French Quarter to sate a vampire enthusiast's cravings for a more gothic, bohemian lifestyle. Voodoo, witch and vampire shops can be found throughout the neighborhood. Securing a job at one of these shops allows an individual to be surrounded on a daily basis with the environment they enjoy, while sharing their knowledge of these items with tourists as they make their sales. It is no wonder that the French Quarter has such an eclectic feel. From artists to musicians to vampires, the French Quarter has something for everyone.

Anne Rice, with *Interview with the Vampire*, created a seductive version of New Orleans as a vampire mecca. People started coming to New Orleans looking for a vampire experience, which spawned the popular Anne Rice's Vampire Lestat Fan Club Halloween Balls. Suzie Quiroz, one of the original founders of the fan club, in addition to Melanie Scott, Teresa Simmons and Susie Miller, started the club almost thirty years ago. Quiroz served as Anne Rice's personal assistant for fifteen years and continues to produce the balls for Lestat and Anne Rice fans. "People from all walks of life have a little vampire in them," said Quiroz. "We find that attendees to our events, anyone from serious vampire role players, to individuals who just identify with Anne's very three dimensional and somewhat romantic characterization of vampires, enjoy escaping into their world for just one night."

French Quarter tour companies soon found it feasible to add dedicated vampire tours to their mix of ghost and cemetery tours, which already flourished as an entertainment source for tourists. "We found more and more that on our ghost tours, customers would ask us about New Orleans vampires," said Sidney Smith, owner of Haunted History Tours. "We quickly found that there were ample tourists with an interest in vampires, that adding a tour strictly on vampires made sense." Smith also discovered that finding tour guides to lead these tours was not difficult. "Many of our tour guides are themselves intrigued with the vampire creature, making this a fun tour for everyone." Sidney went on to explain that presenting this tour has its own challenges, however. "The tour guides that we use on that particular tour have to be VERY knowledgeable about the subject matter, because many of the vampire tour participants are quite knowledgeable themselves about vampires, and will 'test' the guide's knowledge. Or, they simply take the tour to have fun and learn even more about the vampire culture in New Orleans."

Several vampire-themed and gothic nightclubs sprouted up in the French Quarter as well. The Dungeon, located on Toulouse Street, just off of Bourbon, was famous for opening at midnight prior to the Katrina Hurricane, making it spooky and mysterious. A small door serves as an entrance to a long alleyway that leads to the club. Still in existence today, the club now opens much earlier but still has a gothic atmosphere, perfect for those in search of somewhere a vampire might cocktail. Some clubs have come and gone, such as the Morgue and Mythique, which were both very popular among local vampire enthusiasts. However, many have taken their place, proving the ongoing desire for this type of venue for both locals and tourists alike. The Toulouse Dive Bar, located just next to the Dungeon, was formerly the front part of the Dungeon. Today, it is a gothic bar, frequented by locals. Tourists who happen to wander into the bar are delighted by its somewhat dark atmosphere and the mysterious bathroom. Other places vampires might frequent are Pirate's Alley Café, a tiny bar located next to the St. Louis Cathedral that specializes in absinthe. The atmosphere of the bar, along with its very location, makes it a favorite among those desiring a vampire experience. It is just such a place one would expect to find a lonely vampire hunting for its next conquest. Lafitte's Blacksmith Shop, located on Bourbon Street at St. Philip, is one of the oldest buildings standing in the French Quarter. When sitting around the dark piano bar in the back of the establishment, one can almost feel the pirates of the past trapped in the walls, making their deals and celebrating their rum. Recently, we opened Potions, a vampire-themed speakeasy and private club as sort of an extension to our vampire shop, Boutique du Vampyre. A password is required in order to be admitted into the club, which can only be obtained at Boutique du Vampyre or through a few vampire tour guides. The enthusiasm from both locals and tourists alike has already been phenomenal, proving that the interest in clubs such as this are desired by those visiting and living in the French Quarter.

Afterword

The Stranger with a Cane, My New Orleans Vampire Experience

Are vampires real? Nobody loves vampires more than I do, but reason and common sense tells me no, they are not. It seems that in this day and age, if vampires did exist, we would certainly know that for sure by now. Although, that being said, I know many well-educated non-superstitious individuals who have had true ghost experiences, yet the existence of spirits continues to be a topic of questionability across the world. It is difficult to believe the existence of ghosts until one has crossed your path. So, with that in mind, maybe, just maybe, vampires have lingered in the shadows successfully so as not to be found out. Maybe they have been just careful enough to survive, only occasionally slipping up, exposing themselves to the mortal world, but then quickly returning to the shadows. Every culture has a unique version of the creature that survives on blood and lives forever. Most legends do come from some truth. Perhaps the creature we know as vampire somehow lives among us yet has been careful enough to remain a mystery.

While everything in my intellect tells me that vampires are certainly a myth, still, on many, many nights when I work in my shop alone, making candles late into the night, my back turned to the front door, the hair on my neck stands at end in anticipation of a man entering the shop—a strange man with a cane who appeared at the very first location of our little vampire shop, not long after we opened. I know deep in my heart that I will see this man one day again. Why that is, I have no idea.

I opened Boutique du Vampyre on January 1, 2003. It took me forever to find a location, so, getting frustrated, I finally settled on what I thought might be an okay spot. The first shop, 726 Orleans, is smack in the heart of the French Quarter and only steps from Bourbon Street. However, the structure of the property for a boutique was less than attractive. There was a long carriageway one had to enter and walk through that dead ended into a very large mirror. Then to the right were two steps up into my shop. I thought it might just be creepy and mysterious enough to be the perfect entrance for a vampire shop. However, the mystery and inaccessibility kept most tourists out.

The front room was very large, with two nice-sized windows looking out to Orleans Street. There was a large, dramatic fireplace on the wall opposite the door. The shop consisted of just one large room, while additional private working space was just out of site. Formerly constructed as an apartment, the kitchen was to the left, which we converted into our candle studio, where we crafted our fortune candles daily. There was another door that led to the bathroom and what would have been the bedroom, which we used for storage.

The shop was located just behind the St. Louis Cathedral, across from the busy Bourbon Orleans Hotel. Between Royal and Bourbon Streets, it really should have been a high traffic location, but that unfortunately was not the case. We started with just a few products, the most unusual, our fortune candles. We crafted them ourselves and placed little metal charms throughout them. When a customer was interested in purchasing one, they would be asked several personality questions, and we would select the appropriate candle for them so that when the charms were revealed, each charm would have a specific meaning for the customer. So, with an optimistic attitude, we made candles every day and also added little unusual items to our product mix, which local artists brought us from time to time.

Once in the kitchen, or candle studio, it was impossible to see the front room, making it difficult to know if someone had entered. However, my German Shepherd, Elke, came to work with me daily and was my alert when a customer came into the store. Elke was a very sweet dog. Large for a female, with a long jet-black coat, she looked menacing but was actually a very gentle soul. I could see Elke from my vantage point in the kitchen. She would be lying next to my desk by the fireplace. If a customer walked in, Elke would sit up, and I knew someone was there. She was twelve years old at the time. Very mature, intelligent and reasonable, she enjoyed company but also wanted to make sure I was completely aware when someone had entered our space.

On one very strange evening, things with Elke were not the same. I had been in the candle studio for some time setting up the molds, picking out the metal charms we put inside them and melting the wax. What was about to transpire was so bizarre that every single detail is clearly ingrained in my mind to this day.

Just as I was pouring the wax into the candle molds, Elke stood up and started to growl. This was so unusual that it made me anxious, and I finished the pour as quickly as possible. I could hear someone enter the store, someone who walked with a cane. It was a distinct sound. I told Elke to stop growling, but at the same time, I was concerned, as that was not her normal behavior. I wasn't scared; I was just embarrassed and didn't want the customer to be frightened. I thought it was most likely the cane that was disturbing her. Perhaps she found it threatening. I hurried out as fast as I could and made my way to Elke and the customer.

If vampires existed, the man who stood at the entrance of our shop had the persona. He did not by any means appear to be in costume as a vampire tour guide might be: dressed in elaborate Victorian garb, with made-up eyes and piercings, ready to play the part. No, this man, while dressed in all black, wore what appeared to be expensive tailored pants and a dress shirt, as they fit his slender, tall build to perfection. I tried to tell myself that he looked Greek, or Italian, so not to sound cliché, but truth be told, he appeared to me to be what I would consider Romanian. His cane was elaborate. An ornate silver handle was attached to a lovely wooden stick, and he maneuvered about the room with grace, much to Elke's dislike.

While I was petting Elke's head, I felt the grumbling vibration of her low, almost silent growl continue. She felt threatened by him, something I had never seen in her twelve years. I continued to stroke her head and quietly told her to sit, but she would have no part of that. She stood to protect. The man made his way around the shop. Nervous, I greeted him as I would any customer, explaining that everything in the shop was hand crafted for us. I explained the fortune candles to him, all the while feeling Elke's growl beneath my hand. It was the most unsettling feeling I have ever encountered. Meanwhile, he completely ignored me. He never looked in my direction. He seemed not to care one bit what I was painfully explaining to him. Then, when he got to the small bookcase, he said, "Do you have the history of the vampire?"

I was so pleased that he finally spoke, and I almost knew what he would sound like before any words had come out of his mouth. He spoke with what sounded like a Romanian accent—not put on by any means, but a true accent he did not care if I noticed or not.

"No, we don't," I quickly stuttered out. "I only carry books that are signed by the authors." My voice shook, and it embarrassed me. "But that's a good idea. I'll have to consider that." I was so nervous and somehow wanted his approval. He did not seem disappointed but maybe a little annoyed. He had only looked at me briefly and then continued walking around the room, when he said one last thing—and it was more to himself than to me. "I know people who would be very interested in this." At that point I started to talk, but I have no idea what I was saying. I was probably trying to take his comment as a compliment, thinking he was pleased by what he saw. I was trying to smooth things between us over, as I felt he didn't care for me one bit. I didn't really think he was happy with the items in my shop at all. I think he was intrigued with the idea of the shop in general. Had he been a vampire, he might have considered it a compliment to himself.

He took a few more moments walking about, and then he walked out of the shop as slowly as he had been walking around it. He never looked back at me or seemed to care at all that I was there. As he took the two steps down, out of the shop and into the carriageway, I simultaneously sat down, as did Elke. I patted her head, and as I said the words "That was weird," I saw Steve, my boyfriend at the time, now my husband, walking by the windows in front of the shop. He walks with purpose, so my peripheral vision caught his presence immediately. I was so pleased, as I knew Steve would basically be entering the carriageway as this man with the cane was exiting. It would have been impossible for them not to meet at the street entrance. This way Steve would know exactly who I was talking about. However, when Steve walked in, I mentioned the strange man who had just left. Steve shrugged his shoulders and said that no one had just come from the shop. It had been an extremely slow day, as was the norm at that time. Traffic on the street in general was sparse. I argued with Steve briefly and reiterated that the strange man had just vacated the store. I got no response, so I bolted past Steve, down the carriageway and out the gate, only seconds after the man had left. There was not a soul on the street in either direction. Whether someone walked with a cane or not, it would have been impossible for anyone to disappear that quickly in any direction.

Steve never understood my anxiety with or fascination about the situation. I say that's only because he did not get to meet the stranger with the cane. That unusual encounter haunts me to this day. I think what haunts me more is my absolute certainty that he will once again appear at Boutique du Vampyre. Now in a wonderful location for business at 709½ St. Ann, our shop has since that time grown in leaps and bounds. Above all things we offer the history of the vampire.

Bibliography

Anderson, Julie, Emm Barnes, and Enna Shackleton. *The Art of Medicine: Over 2,000 Years of Images and Imagination*. Lewes, UK: Ilex Press Limited, 2013.

Arthur, Stanley C., and Roger Baudier. "The Casket Girls." Archdiocesan Archives, n.d.

Blumenthal, Walter Hart. *Brides from Bridewell*. Westport, CT: Greenwood, 1973.

Clark, Emily. *Masterless Mistresses: The New Orleans Ursulines and the Development of a New World Society, 1727–1834*. Chapel Hill: University of North Carolina Press, 2012.

———. *Voices from an Early American Convent*. Baton Rouge: Louisiana State University Press, 2009.

Fortier, Alcee. *A History of Louisiana*. Vol. 1. N.p.: First Rate Publishers, 2016.

Fuller, Jean Overton. *The Comte de Saint Germain*. London: East West Publications, 1988.

Gerard, Emily. *The Land Beyond the Forest*. Cambridge: Cambridge University Press, 2011.

Hall, Manly O. *The Most Holy Trinosophia of Le Comte De St. Germain*. London: Aziloth Books, 2011.

Harpe, Bernard de La, and Glenn R. Conrad, eds. *Historical Journal of the Establishment of the French in Louisiana*. N.p.: 1971.

Heaney, Sister Jane Frances. *A Century of Pioneering*. New Orleans, LA: Ursuline Sisters of New Orleans, 1993.

Levi, Eliphas. *The History of Magic*. Cambridge: Cambridge University Press, 2013.

McWilliams, Richebourg Gaillard. *Fleur de Lys and Calumet*. Tuscaloosa: University of Alabama Press, 2011.

Miller, Richard, and Iona Millier. *The Modern Alchemist*. Grand Rapids, MI: Phanes Press, 1994.

Oakley, Isabel Cooper. *The Comte de St. Germain*. New York: Rudolph Steiner, 1970.

Prophet, Elizabeth Clare. *Saint Germain—Master Alchemist*. Livingston, MT: Summit University Press, 2004.

"The Rise and Fall of John Law." *Historic New Orleans Collection Quarterly* 28, no. 4 (Fall 2011): 2–9.

Smith, Kalila. *New Orleans Ghosts, Voodoo and Vampires*. New Orleans, LA: DeSimonin Publications, 1997.

Waggoner, May Rush Gwin, ed. *Le Plus Beau Pais Du Monde—Completing the Picture of Proprietary Louisiana, 1699–1722*. Lafayette: Center for Louisiana Studies, 2005.

Widmer, Mary Lou. *New Orleans in the Thirties*. Gretna, LA: Pelican Publishing Company, 1989.

Index

About the Author

Photo by Linda Minutola Raymond.

Marita Woywod Crandle has been writing and storytelling since she was a little girl. She has always had a fancy for the magical side of life, making New Orleans, with its very creative atmosphere, a perfect match for this German transplant. Marita is currently working on a novel dedicated to one of the French Quarter legends, the Carter Brothers, and the book *Drinking Mistakes*, her memoirs as a Bourbon Street bartender. Marita has also written the holiday children's book *Rufus, the Yuletide Bat*, available at her gift store.

Marita is married to Steven Crandle of New Orleans, and together they run the Boutique du Vampyre and their private vampire nightclub, Potions. Marita has a passion for animals and has rescued over 650 dogs since she has moved to the French Quarter. She and her husband currently live both in the French Quarter and in Lake Front with their three rescued German Shepherds—Turbo Dog, Vilma and Atlas—and their rescued cockatiel, Voodoo.

Visit us at
www.historypress.net

This title is also available as an e-book

Printed in the USA
CPSIA information can be obtained
at www.ICGtesting.com
LVHW082035041123
762998LV00006B/535